A CONSTRUCTIVE THEOLOGY OF
INTELLECTUAL DISABILITY

A Constructive Theology of Intellectual Disability

HUMAN BEING AS MUTUALITY AND RESPONSE

Molly C. Haslam

Fordham University Press

NEW YORK ‡ 2012

Library of Congress Cataloging-in-Publication Data

Haslam, Molly Claire.
A constructive theology of intellectual disability : human being as mutuality and response / Molly C. Haslam. — 1st ed.
    p. cm.
Includes bibliographical references (p.   )
ISBN 978-0-8232-3940-5 (cloth : alk. paper) —
ISBN 978-0-8232-3941-2 (pbk. : alk. paper)
1. Theological anthropology—Christianity. 2. Human beings. 3. Mental retardation—Religious aspects—Christianity. 4. People with mental disabilities—Religious life. I. Title.
BT732.4.H37 2012
233'.5—dc23   2011026671

Printed in the United States of America
14 13 12   5 4 3 2 1
First edition

To my parents, Don and Claire, without whose love and support this book would not have been possible

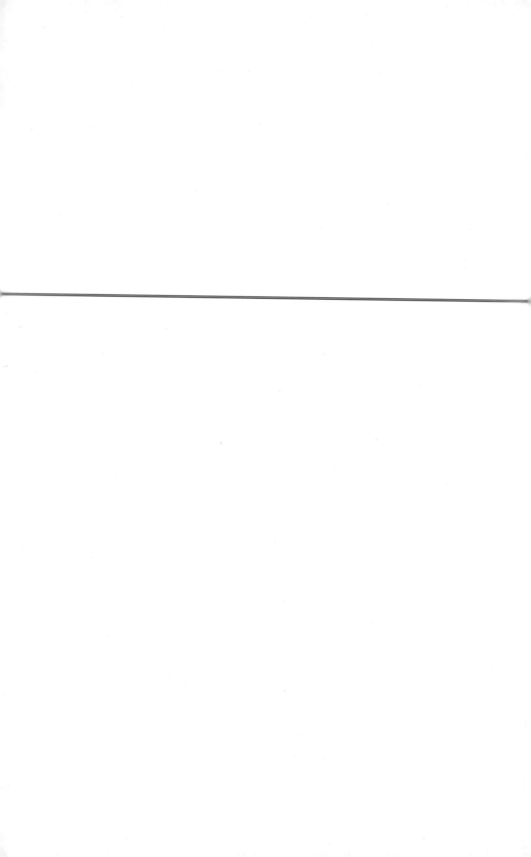

CONTENTS

Introduction 1

1. Gordon Kaufman: Human Being as Intentional Agent 19
2. George Lindbeck: Human Being as Language User 36
3. Human Being in Relational Terms: A Phenomenology 53
4. Martin Buber's Anthropology 67
5. *Imago Dei* as Rationality or Relationality:
   History and Construction 92

Notes 117
Bibliography 131

A CONSTRUCTIVE THEOLOGY OF INTELLECTUAL DISABILITY

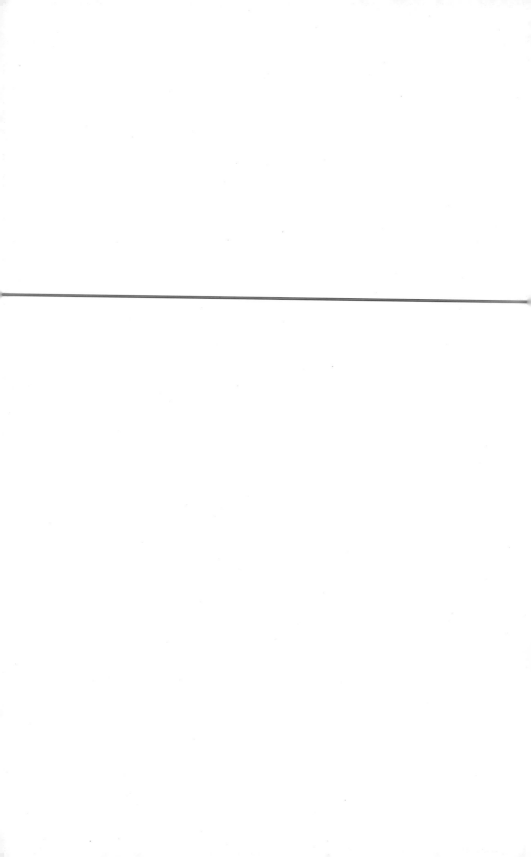

Introduction

PEOPLE WITH DISABILITIES in the United States have been
mobilizing for more than a century in the struggle to overcome
injustice and oppression. In 1850, deaf people established local
organizations to advocate for their interests. During the Depression,
the League of the Physically Handicapped organized sit-ins and picket
lines at federal offices to protest discrimination against people with
disabilities in employment and in New Deal social welfare programs.
In the 1940s, the National Federation of the Blind was established,
and, following World War II, the Paralyzed Veterans of America was
founded.[1] During the 1950s, people with disabilities and their families
formed self-help organizations to lobby governments and to provide
services.[2]

In the 1960s, the contemporary disability rights movement emerged
in the wake of the struggle of African Americans and women for civil
rights. People with disabilities began to identify themselves as a minority group that had been denied basic civil rights such as the right to
vote, to marry and bear children, and to obtain employment. Disabled
people and their advocates began calling on the same constitutional
clauses for court victories and legislative changes achieved in movements by these other disadvantaged groups.[3] In the years that followed,
a number of significant political and legislative changes were made.
Among these changes include the passage of the Rehabilitation Act of
1973, which safeguarded the civil rights of people with disabilities.
It was the first major comprehensive civil rights law for people with
disabilities in the United States. In 1990, Congress passed the
landmark Americans with Disabilities Act, which mandated equal
access for people with disabilities to employment, public facilities and
services, public accommodations, and telecommunications.[4]

Yet, despite the many victories accomplished by individuals with disabilities and their advocates over the years, injustice remains. People with disabilities continue to face architectural and attitudinal barriers that limit their full participation in society. Thus, the work of the disability rights movement continues, at all levels of personal and political life.

As with most civil rights movements, the disability rights movement in the late 1960s resulted in a dramatic increase in publications addressing the concerns of individuals with disabilities. In most fields of study, titles emerged reflecting the growing awareness of these concerns. In Christian theology, however, theoretical works addressing disability appeared much later on the scene. It was not until the mid-1990s that Nancy Eiesland's landmark book *The Disabled God: Toward a Liberatory Theology of Disability* was published.[5] Though the number of publications remains small, theorizing on behalf of individuals with disabilities is taking place in an effort to address their position as full participants in the life of the church and the wider community.

A significant problem remains, however, in that the bulk of theorizing on disability in Christian theology addresses almost exclusively the concerns of those with physical disabilities, and little attention is given to the status of those with intellectual disabilities. Nancy Eiesland admits this when she writes, "the paucity of theological exploration of social, emotional, and intellectual disabilities is scandalous."[6] Though Eiesland's aim in her book is to develop an understanding of God that is relevant exclusively to the concerns of those with physical disabilities, she calls upon her readers to engage in theological work that addresses the unique concerns of those with intellectual disabilities.

In recent years, a few works have emerged that address this paucity of engagement with individuals with intellectual disabilities in Christian theology: Thomas E. Reynolds's *Vulnerable Communion: A Theology of Disability and Hospitality*, Amos Yong's *Theology and Down Syndrome: Reimagining Disability in Late Modernity*, and Hans Reinders's *Receiving the Gift of Friendship: Profound Disability, Theological Anthropology, and Ethics*. Each of these works addresses the status of individuals with intellectual disabilities in Christian theology and assumes the task of reconstructing concepts of God, Christ, and human being in ways that are life-giving for these individuals. This increase in attention to individuals with intellectual disabilities in Christian theology is a hopeful sign that more theorizing with these individuals in mind is yet to come. A significant problems remains, however, in that, while each work provides valuable insights into the nature of religious concepts vis-à-vis some individuals with intellectual disabilities, each in various ways betrays a bias toward a level of intellectual ability unavailable to individuals with profound intellectual disabilities.

It is ironic that this bias appears in works written with the intention of promoting the well-being of individuals with intellectual disabilities in the church and society, but this problem has no reflection on the intentions of the theologians. The bias toward intellectual ability is intractable and so deeply rooted in Western philosophy and Christian theology that it appears in all areas of intellectual activity. In this book, I seek to redress this problem as it appears in Christian theology and attempt to construct an understanding of human being and the *imago Dei* that is life-giving for individuals with profound intellectual disabilities. This is a daunting task, for I am aware of my own rooted-ness in Western philosophy and its privileging of the rational, thinking aspects of the human person. However, I am also mindful of the many individuals with profound intellectual disabilities who have touched my life over the years and the profound joy I have experienced in relationship with them. Their status as human beings or images of God has never been in doubt for me, and I have been deeply troubled by the prevalence in Christian theology of concepts that ignore their full participation in all aspects of life. Thus, I forge ahead in hope that this work will assist in weakening the bias toward the thinking, rational self in Christian theology and contribute to the development of religious concepts that promote the well-being of individuals with profound intellectual disabilities.

While not writing exclusively with individuals with intellectual disabilities in mind, Thomas E. Reynolds indicates his intention to develop a theology of vulnerability that is inclusive of individuals with intellectual disabilities, in particular, individuals with autism spectrum disorders.[7] Reynolds's goal in *Vulnerable Communion* is to construct a concept of human community that is welcoming of the stranger, not as a spectacle but as someone with inherent value, created in the image of God.[8] In order to accomplish this, he claims, we need "a moral vision of the person that can marshal our collective energies and projects in the service of human flourishing."[9] Reynolds employs a metaphorical reversal here and conceives of human being no longer as autonomous and self-sufficient, but rather as "agents identified by the relationships we have with others."[10] Reynolds privileges disability here, and he suggests that what is basic to human being is vulnerability versus strength, lack of ability versus ability, and dependence on others from whom we receive our existence versus independence and self-sufficiency.

Thus far, Reynolds's conception of human being is inclusive of individuals with profound intellectual disabilities, for they are surely vulnerable in their limited ability and dependence on others for meeting their most basic needs. What becomes problematic is Reynolds's further claim that it is not enough merely to state as a fact that we are all vulnerable and disabled; we must go farther and acknowledge this reality.[11] For Reynolds, this is part and parcel of what it means to love: by being subject to another's vulnerability, I am brought to an awareness of my own vulnerability and thus disposed toward the other with availability and attentiveness to the preciousness of the other by way of sympathy.[12] Reynolds goes farther here and identifies this capacity for availability and "response-ability" with the *imago Dei*. We image God in our capacity to respond to God and others, which for Reynolds entails "the freedom to self-consciously acknowledge and enter into relationships."[13] We image God, Reynolds suggests, in that we are "self-conscious, aware of our bodies, able to call this particular body mine vis-à-vis other bodies."[14]

Conceiving of the *imago Dei* relationally, in terms of responsiveness to the world around us, as Reynolds does, is an important first step toward the development of a theological anthropology that is life-giving for individuals with profound intellectual disabilities. What is problematic with Reynolds's account, however, is that this responsiveness takes a turn toward the agential self, such that participation in the *imago Dei* requires the intellectual capacity to conceive of the self as distinct from the world around us. For Reynolds, we image God in that, through our capacities for self-consciousness, we respond to the other with respect, fidelity, and compassion.[15] As I will indicate in the coming pages, this tendency to emphasize the self-conscious, agential self is prevalent in Christian theology and requires that we go further in our reconstructive efforts if we are to develop a theological anthropology that is life-giving for individuals with profound intellectual disabilities.

In *Theology and Down Syndrome*, Amos Yong constructs a "pneumatological theology of disability."[16] This theology is informed and shaped by the Christian experience of the Holy Spirit and the biblical narratives of the Holy Spirit—what Yong names "the pneumatological imagination." For Yong, the pneumatological imagination alerts us to discern the activity of the Holy Spirit not only in the "tongues" of the diversity of academic discourses and scientific disciplines, but also in the experiences of individuals with Down syndrome and other disabilities.[17]

With attention to a variety of disabilities, Yong constructs an anthropology of interrelationality or interdependence, which includes relationships involving non-self-conscious persons (interpersonal relations) as well as relationships involving self-consciously engaged persons (intersubjective relations). Yong turns to the caregiver relationship here and claims that the dignity of the individual lacking in rational capacity is "attached" to the dignity of the caregiver. So, such a person is worthy not because of a capacity she may or may not have, but because "she is a being who has become who she is through the loving care of a mothering person—a person who herself embodies intrinsic worth."[18] Attaching the worth of an individual with a profound intellectual disability to the dignity of a caregiver is beneficial when that caregiver is responding to the individual with respect and concern. What happens, though, when the caregiver is having a particularly bad day? Perhaps she finds herself unable to respond with dignity, in loving or caring ways. Does the individual with the disability lose his or her dignity in these circumstances? Yong moves outside of the individual with the disability here and places human dignity not in some capacity possessed by the individual, but in the nature of responsiveness toward her on the part of others with whom she is in relation.

Other theologians have made a similar move. I am thinking of Hans Reinders in particular here, whose work I will address momentarily. For now, suffice it to say that understanding the dignity of individuals with profound intellectual disabilities in terms of the dignity of a caregiver is highly concerning given that, unfortunately, these relationships can be lacking in dignity, abusive, and neglectful.

Yong goes on to address the meaning of human being as created in the image of God. For Yong, we participate in the *imago Dei* insofar as we participate in relationships of friendship.[19] He writes, "the power of friendship is precisely that self-sacrificial mutuality emerges apart from what friends think they may gain from their relationships," and "friendship manifests commitment and mutual valuation."[20] The question here becomes this: In what way does this notion of friendship apply to individuals with profound intellectual disabilities? In what way may they participate in the image of God given that the behavior of these individuals does not express the capacity for self-awareness necessary to sacrifice for another, commit to another, or valuate another? In his discussion of friendship, Yong does briefly add "and genuine interpersonal relations are possible even with people with severe and profound intellectual disabilities,"[21] but he does not clarify how their participation in these relationships can fulfill the requirements of self-sacrificial mutuality, commitment, and mutual valuation he considers necessary for imaging God.

As in the case of Reynolds, I find Yong's use of a relational understanding of the *imago Dei* helpful as a starting point for the development of a theological anthropology that is life-giving for individuals with profound intellectual disabilities. However, Yong's understanding of the *imago Dei* as participation in relationship in terms of friendships that involve self-sacrifice, mutual valuation, and commitment indicates once again a bias toward the agential self with the intellectual capacity to conceive of self and other necessary to act with intention in the world around him or her. If we are to develop a theological anthropology that promotes the flourishing of all human beings, including those among us with profound intellectual disabilities, then we must go farther in our reconstructive efforts, beyond our dependence upon an agential view of the human person, to develop an understanding of what it means to image God that is inclusive of individuals with profound intellectual disabilities.

To my knowledge, Hans Reinders's *Receiving the Gift of Friendship* is the first book to address directly the question of what it means to be human and created in the image of God with respect to individuals with profound intellectual disabilities.[22] Reinders states clearly that his goal is not the construction of a theology of disability. Rather, it is to "contribute to the development of Christian anthropology in a post-modern age."[23] This is an important distinction because, for Reinders, the most fundamental question is not about how people with disabilities regard themselves, nor is it about how "we" regard "them." Rather, the primary question is how we, "the readers and writers of books," regard ourselves. It is our response to this question, he claims, that will determine "whether or not we are the kind of people who want to share our lives with disabled persons."[24]

Like Reynolds and Yong, Reinders affirms the move in theology toward defining human being in terms of relationality versus the possession of a particular capacity, including the capacity for agency. Grounding our understanding of human being in some capacity possessed by the individual produces the problem of inclusion and exclusion based on ability. Because this capacity has traditionally been conceived in terms of intellectual ability, substance-based anthropologies typically involve the exclusion of individuals with limited intellectual ability. Thus, the move away from a substantialist view toward a relational understanding of the human being is a necessary first step toward the development of a theological anthropology that includes and sustains individuals with profound intellectual disabilities.[25]

The value we receive from Reinders's book lies in his awareness that a second step beyond the move toward a relational anthropology is necessary if we are to construct an understanding of human being that promotes the flourishing of all human beings, including individuals with profound intellectual disabilities.[26] As I have noted in the case of Reynolds and Yong, it is not enough to make this relational turn if our understanding of what it means to participate in relationships requires the intellectual capacity to conceive of the self as distinct from the world around her. In both cases, the specter of the agential self returns, although now under the guise of responding to the other "with respect, fidelity and compassion"[27] and friendships of mutual self-sacrifice, valuation, and commitment.[28] Surely these are virtues worthy of our attention. In my critique of Reynolds and Yong, I am not denying this to be true. Rather, I am agreeing with Reinders that in the development of an understanding of human being and the *imago Dei* that promotes the flourishing of all human beings, including individuals with profound intellectual disabilities, a second step beyond the move toward a relational understanding of human being is necessary.

For Reinders, the necessary second step is "to argue that being human in relationship is grounded extrinsically, that is, 'from outside.'"[29] Reinders turns to theology here and claims that human being in relationship is "dependent on God's continuing act of love toward us."[30] Again, he writes, "God's act of love constitutes being human both with regard to its origin and to its final destination, which logically entails that this relationship is inaugurated by divine action, not human action."[31] Reinders's second step involves God's movement toward us, and thus the human person remains passive in this scenario: "We find ourselves at the receiving end of the act of unconditional divine self-giving."[32] All people, regardless of their opportunities or abilities, receive this gift of God's friendship and are thereby drawn into communion with God and with others.[33]

For Reinders, grounding our understanding of human being "outside" the self, in God's movement toward us, eliminates the problem so prevalent in Christian theology of understanding human being in terms of a capacity internal to the self, rational or otherwise.[34] Furthermore, Reinders notes, arguing from our understanding of God to our understanding of human being is the logically prior task given the Christian understanding of human beings created in the image of God.[35] Two concerns arise, however, with regard to Reinders's second move, "outside" the self. First, if we understand God in agential terms, as Reinders does, as the pursuer in this relationship with passive human beings, in what way does human being image this agential God? Reinders claims that we image God in that we are all participants in God's relationship with us, regardless of our capacities.[36] We are all passive recipients of God's gift of friendship toward us. But, the question remains: In what way does human passivity image this divine agency? There is an inconsistency here that needs clarification. While I appreciate Reinder's efforts to construct an understanding of the human person by eliminating the emphasis on capacities, the move outside the self toward God understood in agential terms raises once again the specter of agency and of capacities inaccessible to individuals with profound intellectual disabilities. Second, Reinders's conception of God as "outside" the world creates a cosmological dualism that is problematic for many who possess a modern concept of the universe. As the theologian Gordon Kaufman reminds us, the advance of science has taught us that to speak of God as a reality that is somehow "outside" the world is to speak of what we cannot know; it is to speak in superstitious terms.[37] Reinders's understanding of God and human being as *imago Dei* remains problematic for those individuals who are mindful of the advances of science and seek to understand God in this-worldly terms.

Thus, in this project I propose an altogether different move in the construction of a theological anthropology that is life-giving for individuals with profound intellectual disabilities. Rather than turn "inside" the self and ground our concept of human being in a particular capacity, or rather than turn "outside" the human being and construct a theological anthropology based on the movement of the other toward us, I suggest that we employ a more holistic understanding of the God/world relation. With the help of Martin Buber's dialogical thought, I suggest that we locate our understanding of human being not on one or the other side of the subject/object dichotomy but in the realm of "the between."[38] We find our humanity in relationships of mutual responsiveness, in which individuals with profound intellectual disabilities participate as responders, albeit in nonsymbolic, nonagential ways. While the behavior of these individuals does not express the ability to employ symbols of self and other necessary to envision a goal and act with intention to achieve it, they do express the ability to respond to the world around them and to evoke a response from others. This is not another capacity-based anthropology. It is not enough simply to have the ability to respond, for mutually responsive relations require the involvement of the other responding in kind. "Human being" is a dynamic, not a static concept, for individuals with profound intellectual disabilities participate as responders in these relationships and not as passive recipients of acts of love toward them.

My concern for the status of the individuals with profound intellectual disabilities in society is long-standing. As a physical therapist, I have come to know individuals with profound intellectual disabilities and their families well through my efforts to communicate with them and to advocate for their inclusion in society. As a Christian committed to the life of the church, I have developed friendships with people with profound intellectual disabilities in church communities and through ministry opportunities. However, it has been only in my formation as an academic theologian that I have become aware of the exclusion of the concerns of individuals with profound intellectual disabilities in Christian theology. Thus, my aim in this book is to redress this deficiency.

In particular, I take up the concern of the disability rights movement to acknowledge the social and political aspects of disability, and I apply this concern to the population of individuals with profound intellectual disabilities. The disability rights movement emerged, in part, as a response to the deficiencies of the vocational and medical models of rehabilitation. The vocational model classified disability in economic terms as "an inability to work in one's former employment or as a health-related limitation on the amount or kind of work a person could perform."[39] As a result, government rehabilitation services functioned as an employment agency providing education, employment training, and job contacts. Despite the benefits of these educational and employment services, vocational rehabilitation was inadequate in its efforts to remedy the disadvantages faced by individuals with disabilities, since it did not address the attitudinal and architectural barriers that prevent people with disabilities from being hired for certain jobs.[40] The medical model classified disability as a medical problem in need of a medical solution. Though it promoted the development of important medical advances for people with disabilities, it promoted a dependent, nonparticipatory role on the part of the individual with the disability. It emphasized professional control of the rehabilitation process versus empowerment of the individual with a disability to make decisions regarding his or her own rehabilitation. The primary problem with both models of rehabilitation is that disability is viewed primarily as a problem of the individual that is best addressed by medical treatment, employment, or education, with no attention to barriers attitudinal and architectural—and theological, as I will demonstrate—that contribute to the marginalization of people with disabilities.[41]

In response, the disability rights movement promoted the minority group model of disability, in which individuals with disabilities are viewed as a group that is stigmatized based on a characteristic common to its members. Disability is understood here as a stigmatized social condition needing redress through attitudinal changes and social commitment to equal opportunity for individuals with disabilities, in contrast to the perception of disability as a private, physical, and emotional problem needing treatment by the medical community.[42] This model emphasizes the fact that people with disabilities struggle more because of discriminatory stereotypes that prevent them from reaching their full potential than from physical, intellectual, or emotional characteristics. In this project, I pick up this emphasis on the social aspects of understanding disability and consider the ways in which our theological categories perpetuate this stigmatization of individuals with disabilities.

While I find the minority group model of disability helpful in my efforts to critique religious concepts that are discriminatory against individuals with profound intellectual disabilities, it has its weaknesses. I think in particular of this model's tendency to homogenize the experience of people with disabilities in its efforts to highlight the socially constructed nature of disability. The "problem," according to this model, is not the particular characteristics of an individual but rather the socially constructed, oppressive stereotypes that act as barriers keeping individuals with disabilities from attaining status as equal citizens in society. Thus, attention to the particularities of an individual's experience of disability is minimized. The reality, however, is that individuals with disabilities experience disability differently. For example, someone born with an impairment that limits his ability to walk will likely experience life mobilizing in a wheelchair differently from someone who loses the ability to walk later in life. With regard to individuals with profound intellectual disabilities, their behavior does not indicate the intellectual capacity to employ the concepts necessary to acknowledge themselves as distinct from the world around them. Thus, the idea of "experiencing" disability as such would not apply. We can only infer from their behavior what these individuals may or may not be experiencing and make our best guess. Most certainly, the medical model's suggestion that individuals with disabilities should embrace their disability and focus their attention on battling oppressive stereotypes loses force when it comes to individuals with such profound limitations. Thus, another model of disability is required that will allow us to conceive of disability in a way that is mindful of the unique limitations of individuals with profound intellectual disabilities.

In addition to the minority group model, I find Deborah Creamer's limits model of disability helpful for my purposes. In contrast to the minority group model's tendency to minimize differences with regard to disability, this model "emphasizes reflection on the experience of embodiment in its various formations, including disabled embodiment."[43] There is an appreciation here for the fact that there are many forms of embodiment, disabled or not, and many ways of responding to one's embodiment. In addition, with this model disability is no longer understood in absolute terms, in which one is considered either disabled or nondisabled. Rather disability is understood in all its diversity as a category that applies to all of us, at one time or another. As Creamer puts it, "the limits model begins with the notion of limits as a common, indeed quite unsurprising, aspect of being human."[44] Creamer reminds us that all people are limited in varying degrees, and that there is a diversity of ways in which these limits are lived and experienced. Creamer is careful to note that this model does not negate the value of the medical and minority models. She admits that disability in all its diversity and commonality remains a biological and sociopolitical condition. What is missing, however, is attention to the fact that we all experience limits, that these limits differ, and that these limits are experienced and lived in multitudinous ways.[45]

Creamer's model of disability as limits is helpful for my purposes because it offers the conceptual space to account for the unique situation of individuals with profound intellectual disabilities. As Creamer notes, people are limited in varying degrees. The limitations of individuals with profound intellectual disabilities are varied and unique in that their limitations are often complex, and always profound. There is often a combination of profound physical disability in combination with profound intellectual disability. Thus, while I find the minority group model a helpful resource for critiquing and reconstructing theological concepts that exclude individuals with profound intellectual disabilities, I find in Creamer's model a respect for the manifold forms of embodiment, including the varied forms of embodiment of individuals with profound intellectual disabilities.

In this book, I pick up the strength of both models and consider the ways in which our theological categories perpetuate the stigmatization of individuals with profound intellectual disabilities. With an eye toward the particular population of individuals with profound intellectual disabilities, I critique those theological anthropologies, common to the Christian tradition, in which human being is defined by an intellectual capacity, such as the capacity to engage the world symbolically or to understand God. Such anthropologies, I argue, contribute to the marginalization of individuals with profound intellectual disabilities because these individuals do not possess the intellectual capacities that have traditionally defined human being in Christian theology. Such anthropologies cannot account for the full humanity of these individuals. Thus, I suggest, our concept of human being must be reconceived.

I address in particular the theological anthropologies of Gordon Kaufman and George Lindbeck. I address the theology of Gordon Kaufman because his work has been decisive for constructive, revisionist theology, and I address Lindbeck's theology because of his significant influence on postliberal theology. But, more important, I engage these authors to demonstrate the intractability of the privileging of rationality; even in the work of contemporary theologians who, through the work of liberation theologians have become aware of the power of religious concepts to marginalize certain groups, this bias toward a level of intellectual ability persists. Both theologians claim that the ability to employ symbolic material is an element essential to being considered human, an anthropology that clearly considers as deficiently human those with profound intellectual disabilities for whom the use of language and other symbolic material is not an option. To address this problem, I begin with a detailed analysis of the claims of Lindbeck and Kaufman. I follow with a defense of my counterclaim that the theological anthropology they employ is biased in favor of the intellectually abled, for whom language use is taken for granted. Like the history of thought on the meaning of human being, Lindbeck and Kaufman both employ an understanding of the human as based on some capacity, in this case the intellectual capacity for symbol-use.

Kaufman and Lindbeck come by the tendency to privilege intellectual capacity honestly. Christianity came to life in a culture infused with Neoplatonic philosophy and its privileging of the world of ideas over the material world. Thus, this bias can be found in Christianity's earliest texts, and it persists throughout the history of Christian theology. In an effort to give an historical perspective on the prevalence of intellectualism in Christian theology, I include an analysis of the theology of the *imago Dei* of two classical Christian thinkers, Thomas Aquinas and John Calvin. I demonstrate that they share a bias toward an intellectualist conception of the self, as having the intellectual ability to understand God in the case of Aquinas, or to choose obedience to God's commands in the case of Calvin. I claim that such a conception of the self in the history of Christian thought has serious, detrimental consequences for the lives of those with profound intellectual disabilities, and that academic theology has yet to acknowledge fully the ramifications of its bias toward this rational conception of the self.

I conclude this book by developing a theological anthropology in which human being is defined not in terms of some capacity that she or he may or may not possess. What defines human being is not located internal, or external, to the self but rather is located in the human-to-human relationship and in the relationship of human beings to God. Tellingly, it is primarily academics who ask whether the capacity for reason is necessary to be considered human. Rarely will the mother of a profoundly intellectually disabled child wonder if her child is a human being. Rather, drawing upon my own experience of relationship with individuals with profound intellectual disabilities and their caregivers, I argue that it is in relationships of mutual responsiveness, in which individuals with profound intellectual disabilities participate as communicators, albeit in a nonsymbolic way, that they find their humanity, as do all individuals regardless of capabilities.[46] Thus, to develop this alternative theological anthropology, this book has a narrative component in which I describe my experiences of relationship with individuals with profound intellectual disabilities. What this narrative shows is that individuals with profound intellectual disabilities participate in relationships as responders. They are encountered not as passive recipients of care but as active participants in relationships of mutual responsiveness. I develop as well a phenomenology of the relationality of an individual with a profound intellectual disability, in which I interpret his responsiveness as expressive of his role as a participant in communication, and thereby as expressive of his participation as a human being.

What it means to be human, I argue, is not grounded in some capacity for reasoning, moral or otherwise, for if it were, what would warrant our humane treatment of individuals with profound intellectual disabilities? What would justify the development of social policies that would protect them from neglect and abuse? The *imago Dei* is not located in a capacity for rationality and the freedom to choose (Irenaeus) or in a capacity for understanding and loving God (Aquinas), for if it were, in what way could we as theologians conceive of individuals with profound intellectual disabilities as human beings in the eyes of God? Rather, drawing upon the conception of *imago Dei* in Genesis 1, as well as Martin Buber's *I and Thou*, I argue that our humanity is located in relationships of mutual responsiveness with the Thou we encounter. To be human, for Buber, is to be in relation.[47] To conceive human being in terms of relationality versus capacity offers a conception of the human that is no longer discriminatory of individuals with profound intellectual disabilities. It is to consider these individuals as participating fully in the category "human," as participants in these relationships of mutual responsiveness.

Aside from the narrative component, my method of inquiry for this book is also revisionist and liberationist. It is revisionist in its critical correlation of the situation of individuals with profound intellectual disabilities in society and theology with the traditional Christian understanding of what it means to be human in the eyes of God. Here I use the narrative component as a lens through which I view the limits of conceptions of the human that require rationality, as well as a resource for the development of an alternative theological anthropology that is inclusive of individuals with profound intellectual disabilities.

My method of inquiry is also liberationist in that I intentionally side with individuals with profound intellectual disabilities and their caregivers by acknowledging that Christian theology has excluded them. I acknowledge with Elizabeth Johnson in *She Who Is* that our symbols function and have the power to shape reality. Our religious symbols "legitimate social structures, political arrangements, attitudinal inclinations . . . and visions of what can be."[48] I respond by reexamining the Christian symbol of human being and acknowledge the ways in which it marginalizes individuals with profound intellectual disabilities. I claim that the Christian concept of human being as located in a particular intellectual capacity marginalizes those individuals with profound intellectual disabilities as deficiently human as a result of their disability. Finally, I suggest an alternative theological anthropology that appreciates the full humanity of this population.

Thus, I consider this book to be a liberatory theology of profound intellectual disability disability. For Eiesland, a liberatory theology of disability not only creates new ways of resisting theological symbols that exclude people with disabilities, but it also grounds itself in the bodies and actions of people with disabilities and those who care for them. It is not hierarchical but dialogical or relational in its effort to come from the perspective of the individual with the disability, and not from the individual who is "normally abled."[49] It is for this reason that I include a phenomenology of the relationality of an individual with a profound intellectual disability in this book.

Ideally, in a liberatory theology of disability, individuals with disabilities maintain the speaking center and, if they are not themselves theologians seeking to reconstruct theological symbols, then they remain in close dialogue with the theologian who is. In the case of this liberatory theology of profound intellectual disability, however, it is obviously not possible to participate in dialogue with the individual with profound intellectual disability at the speaking center. Because of their intellectual disability, these individuals are unable to communicate symbolically or linguistically. Thus, I have constructed this liberatory theological anthropology with special attention to the ways in which these individuals communicate in nonsymbolic ways. I have engaged in close observation of their behavior as they engage in relationship with me and their other caregivers, and I have drawn conclusions based upon what I observe. There are dangers in drawing conclusions about the communication of individuals based on observation of bodily behavior only and not symbolic expression. There is the obvious danger that I will project my own idea onto the individual with the profound intellectual disability and get it completely wrong. But what other option do we as caregivers, healthcare workers, or family members of these individuals have besides observing their behavior and making our best guess?

For this population of individuals for whom language-use is not an option, it is up to those who care for them to advocate on their behalf. We run the risk of misinterpreting their behavior, which is a risk common to all human communication, but we have no other choice except to remain silent on the question of whether these individuals participate in being human. To remain silent on this issue, however, is to condone the regnant understanding of human being in intellectual terms. To remain silent is also to condone those social policies that are based on this understanding of human being and thus lead to the neglect and abuse of these individuals. In this book, I have chosen not to remain silent on the question of the humanity of individuals with profound intellectual disabilities, and I have chosen to accept the risk of misinterpretation. It is my hope that this project will be read not as an attempt to provide a final, incontrovertible claim regarding the meaning of "human being." Rather, I hope it will result in further observation of the behavior of these individuals by others who care for them. And I hope it will result in further theorizing on the ways in which these individuals participate in the category "human being" and are thereby deserving of the respect and care this category confers.

I imagine by now some questions have emerged in the reader's mind that are worth addressing before I proceed. Even though I am engaging the unique situation of individuals with profound disabilities in particular in this book, readers might notice themes emerging that would also be relevant in other areas of ethical and theological discourse—the ethical treatment of animals, for example, or infants and individuals in a persistent vegetative state. I intentionally narrowed the population I engage in this book to individuals with profound intellectual disabilities, primarily because the passion that invoked this work grew from my own experience of mutually responsive relationships with these individuals. The persistent discrimination against individuals with profound intellectual disabilities in the theological concepts Christians have employed throughout the centuries, as well as in the practices Christians have performed in our churches and communities, has been greatly troubling to me and fueled my efforts to speak out against it.

As I approached the conclusion of this book, however, I realized the relevance of my constructive proposal for these other groups. I attend to these issues in the conclusion. The possibilities of the theological anthropology proposed in this book for promoting the ethical treatment of these groups are fascinating and worthy of further investigation, and I considered broadening the scope of this project to include them. In the end, however, I decided that to broaden the scope to include these groups would have made this project unwieldy. Addressing the relevance of this project for each of these groups would be a complex task, and each would be deserving of the focused attention with which this book was written. In addition, to include adequate treatment of these other concerns would have detracted from my primary concern of promoting the awareness of individuals with profound intellectual disabilities as worthy of the respect and care that all who receive the moniker "human being" receive. I hope the reader will not interpret my decision to remain focused on individuals with profound intellectual disabilities as an indication of my lack of concern for these other groups. On the contrary, I am deeply concerned about the ways in which these groups are marginalized in our churches and in society at large, and I hope to include them in future projects. I hope as well that this work will provoke the interest in many others to take up the task of theorizing on behalf of those with limited intellectual abilities.

1. Gordon Kaufman: Human Being as Intentional Agent

FOR GORDON KAUFMAN, theology is work of the human imagination. It is not a description of how things "really" are. We have no direct access to the referent of our concept of God, and thus we have no way of determining the accuracy of our representations of God. Similarly, with the concepts of world and human being, we cannot get outside of our place within the world or our place within humanity in order to encounter the world or the human being as objects for examination.[1] Thus, our aim in theological work, as Kaufman sees it, is not the determination of whether our theological concepts fit reality. It is the construction of theological concepts that get us where we want to go—concepts that provide us with adequate orientation in life.[2] It is human work "emerging out of faith's own need for more adequate orientation and symbolization."[3]

Where, one is moved to ask, does Kaufman assume we would want to go in our theological work? What is it that determines whether our orientation and symbolization are adequate? Kaufman does not depart from tradition here. The construction of theological concepts and symbols that provide adequate orientation for human life is based on those concepts and symbols already inherited from the culture within which the theologian is located, with its religious traditions, myths, rituals, taboos, and linguistic classifications. However, there are times in which the work of the theologian draws attention to what has previously been unrecognized by the tradition.[4] At this point, the theologian engages in the construction of new concepts of God, world, and human being.[5] Such theological work must have comprehensiveness to it. In order to construct concepts that provide orientation for human life, it must engage a broad spectrum of experience. "No important dimension of experience can be omitted, and he or she must exert every effort to root out one-sidedness, prejudice and bias."[6] With adequate attention to the broad range of human experiences, it is possible that the theologian will realize the inadequacy of traditional religious symbols and concepts and will reconstruct those that are meaningful for our time. Thus, one important criterion for Kaufman in determining the adequacy of our religious symbols is the degree to which our symbols reflect an understanding of God, world, and human being that is appropriate to the broad spectrum of human experiences and as a result provides an understanding of human life that is meaningful.

In this chapter, I explore Kaufman's construction of the theological concept "human being" and the degree to which this construction does or does not fulfill his requirement of appropriateness to human experience and the provision of meaning for human life, particularly as this relates to individuals with profound intellectual disabilities. His concept of the human can be found explicitly from his early work in *Systematic Theology* to his more recent *In Face of Mystery*. As I will demonstrate, Kaufman's theological anthropology is developed primarily around an understanding of the human as agent, with capacities for symbol-use, intentionality, self-reflection, creativity, and purposeful action. While he avers that there is no "essence" to human being—no reified point at which the theologian locates "human being"—he himself locates what is essential to human being in the capacity to "grasp, shape, create" itself in and through historical processes—what Kaufman refers to as our "biohistoricity."[7] This concept is one of his most distinctive contributions to theological anthropology. For Kaufman, humans are biological beings in their interconnection with and interdependence upon other forms of life. But they are also historical beings because they are both created by the historical processes that precede them as well as endowed with the power to transform those historical processes toward the development of a new cultural and symbolical world.[8] Humans are historical beings with the capacity for self-reflection necessary to set goals and to act purposefully to attain them.[9] Kaufman claims that this biohistorical understanding of the human is inclusive of the variety of concepts of human existence because, by definition, it includes the capacity to create different understandings of the nature of the human.[10]

Without question, Kaufman's efforts to develop an anthropology that respects our various efforts to understand ourselves as humans are commendable. It is his historicist efforts to avoid an essentialist notion of human being and to appreciate the particular that I find most valuable about Kaufman's theological method. These factors are among the primary reasons that I engage Kaufman's work in this project. His historicist efforts serve as a model for me of theological work that seeks to avoid the oppressive, discriminatory consequences of essentialist claims.

I have hinted at the notion of essentialism here and the power of essentialist claims to oppress. This concept deserves greater treatment, as it is a theme that will resurface in subsequent discussions in this book. The roots of the term go back to ancient Greek philosophers who distinguished the "essence" of a thing from its "accidental" properties. The essence of an object or a person is that which is considered fundamental to its nature. Essential properties are inherent in the nature of an object. Thus, unlike accidental properties that may vary over time, essential properties remain unchanged in response to cultural or historical forces. They are also universal in that they inhere in all instances of the object.[11] An essentialist claim, then, has to do with naming that property of a person or thing that is fundamental, unchanging, and universal in all its instantiations.

It should not be surprising that a number of problems arise when essentialist claims are made. For example, in the case of feminist responses to traditional essentialist claims about women's "nature," problems arise when the complexity of women's experiences is taken into account. Many women do not experience themselves as naturally more intuitive, nurturing, or passive in comparison to men. Such traditional beliefs about the "essential women" are problematic in that they do not take into account the variety of ways women experience themselves. Furthermore, such claims are problematic in that they cannot support radical social change in support of women's equality with men. For example, it would be difficult to promote equal pay for women in the workplace when women are considered "naturally" subordinate to men. Finally, feminists argue that essentialist claims about women's nature are often socially constructed based on notions of sexual difference to justify a traditional division of labor.[12]

Despite the many problems, it is not the case that essentialist claims are necessarily harmful. Returning to the example of feminism, some feminist theorists find essentialist claims about women's nature helpful when the practical concern of supporting the liberation of women and all people are taken into account. They realize that while it is difficult to promote equality with traditional essentialist claims about women's nature, it is equally difficult to promote change with no normative view of human nature and the human good in mind. Thus, these feminists employ essentialist claims in a "strategic" sense.[13] Instead of asking what view of women captures the fundamental, unchanging, universal essence of "women," strategic essentialists ask: What view of women is pragmatic and useful? Strategic essentialists do not seek to define "women" once and for all. Rather, their claims are always practical in nature and open to debate given the changing concerns and voices that are available.[14] I will address essentialism and strategic essentialism further in subsequent chapters, but for now it is important simply to note the dangers of essentialist claims, as well as the possible benefit of such claims made for strategic purposes.

Returning now to Kaufman's anthropology, his commendable efforts to construct an understanding of human being without resorting to essentialist claims elicit a question for me: Has Kaufman succeeded in the development of an anthropology that is inclusive of a variety of concepts of human being and appropriate to a broad spectrum of human experiences? I will argue that he has not. By applying his own efforts to avoid essentialism and to appreciate the diversity of human life, I will demonstrate that Kaufman unwittingly adopts his own essentialist view of human being. Kaufman's concept of the human as biohistorical agent assumes that all human beings possess capacities for agency, self-reflection, and symbol use—capacities that many individuals with profound intellectual disabilities, in fact, do not possess. A logical consequence of this concept of human being is the claim that individuals who do not possess these capacities are deficiently human—a claim I am unwilling to make. Thus, Kaufman's concept of human being as biohistorical is not as inclusive as he supposes. It does not accord full (not deficient) humanity to individuals without capacities for agency, self-reflection, and symbol use. Kaufman's understanding of human being as biohistorical cannot recognize these individuals as fully human because to do so would be to contradict the very premise upon which his claim is based: that it is essential for human beings to possess the ability to grasp, shape, create themselves through their capacities for agency, self-reflection, and symbol-use.

Kaufman's concept of the human as biohistorical agent developed out of his desire to propose a concept that avoids the oppressive consequences of previously essentializing views. He began by taking into account a broad range of human experiences and then sought to develop a concept of human being that respected this diversity. Although the concept that resulted from his efforts is problematic vis-à-vis individuals with profound intellectual disabilities, I find his methodology to be very useful in my efforts to develop a theological anthropology that is mindful of the full humanity of these individuals. Following Kaufman's lead, in this project I take up his criteria that religious concepts reflect a broad spectrum of human experiences and thus provide an understanding of human life that is meaningful, and I argue that human being is defined not by one's capacity for agency, symbol-use, or self-reflection, but rather by one's participation in relationships of mutual responsiveness. Such an understanding of human being takes into account the situation of the profoundly intellectually disabled for whom responsive relations are a possibility but symbol use, agency, and self-reflection are not. As a result, my position avoids the problem of Kaufman's anthropology, which assumes these individuals are deficient human beings. Rather, my position assumes their full humanity. These are individuals who, though they do not communicate intentionally, do have the capacity for responsiveness necessary for relationship at the most basic level.

"HUMAN BEING" IN SYSTEMATIC THEOLOGY

From the very early pages of his *Systematic Theology*, Kaufman's anthropology becomes evident in his treatment of the concept of revelation, which he explicates with the use of the analogy of the human agent as hidden unless revealed. To understand the claim that God has revealed God's self in Christ, Kaufman turns to the analogy of human relationships and the mode of knowledge of persons, which he contrasts with discovery or the mode of knowledge of things. A discovery does not require agency on the part of the object of knowledge. "It presupposes no more than the accessibility of a fundamentally thing-like object of knowledge, an inert reality lying open to our investigation."[15] This mode of knowledge involves activity on the part of the observer, such as observation and measurement, which is guided by the intention of the observer to gain knowledge about the object. The object of this "discovery," however, while it may be active or living, is without such intention or purpose.[16]

By contrast, our knowledge of persons involves more than merely our act of observation and our intention to know them. We gain knowledge of persons primarily through their act of self-revelation. Such an act of self-revelation involves more than acts of an autonomic nature, such as a yawn, or the unintentional movement of a newborn stretching as it wakes from sleep. And Kaufman notes that an act of self-revelation involves more than action intended to hide oneself from another, such as "putting on an act" or "playing a role."[17] Such knowledge involves action with the intention to reveal on the part of the person to be known: "Knowledge of another person depends quite as much on the intention of the one known to reveal himself as it does on the other's intention to know him."[18] This knowledge involves more than mere observation on the part of the knower, and it involves more than simple activity without the intention to reveal. It involves awareness of what would have remained hidden to us had the other chosen not to act, via gesture or word, with the intention to reveal himself or herself. For Kaufman, this model of personal knowledge provides us with an analogue for understanding the concept of revelation. Revelation involves God's act with the intention to unveil in human history what would have otherwise remained hidden.

Kaufman admits that although the concept of divine revelation is implicit in this model of finite interpersonal knowledge, there are important differences between them.[19] God is not one whom we encounter directly, as we do in interpersonal relations. As the Creator and Ground of all that is, it is not possible to conceive of an encounter with God directly in a "revelatory moment."[20] For Kaufman, "revelation" refers not so much to revelatory moments in individual lives but to the total historical process through which God has been revealing God's self. Thus, personal knowledge serves only as an image or analogy with which to understand the concept of the revelation of God, and it is an appropriate one only to the degree that God is known to the Christian community as personal—as one who has and does reveal God's self.[21]

The concept of the human that Kaufman employs here in the development of his concept of revelation is that of the human agent, endowed with the capacity for self-reflection sufficient to establish a goal (self-revealing) and the capacity to act with the intention to achieve it. Such agency requires the intellectual capacity to negotiate the symbols of self and other necessary to set a goal and strive to attain it.[22] And it is this concept of the human that is the analogy upon which Kaufman's image of God as personal agent with the intention to reveal God's self in human history is based. One may ask at this point: In what way is it problematic to conceive God in this way? After all, the capacity for agency is one that most human beings possess. Kaufman is merely drawing upon one of many possible human analogies for the development of his understanding of the God/world relation.

Kaufman's conception of God as analogous to a human agent becomes problematic in his *Systematic Theology* when the analogy functions as that which identifies the ideal human through the doctrine of the *imago Dei*. It is one thing to employ an understanding of human being, albeit an essentialist one, as an image to express in finite terms what is inexpressible any other way—the concept of God, that which monotheistic religions consider to be the source and meaning of all that is. It is quite another to then employ this humanly imaged God to identify a quality considered essential to human being and to name this quality as that which appropriately images the divine.[23]

The doctrine of the *imago Dei* expresses theologically that human beings, though on a finite level, are like God. Traditionally, it has been located in a particular aspect of human being, that is, the gift of reason or the immortality of the soul.[24] For Kaufman, however, the *imago Dei* is defined in terms of humanity's historicity, which he defines as both being made by history and creating and furthering history.[25]

We are what we are because of the unnumbered decisions of those who precede us in ages past, the decisions we have made which shape who we will become, and our capacity to make choices that create and shape the future.[26] For Kaufman, it is this understanding of human being as intrinsically historical in nature that locates the *imago Dei*. The *imago Dei* conceived as humanity's historicity is more than an attribute or feature of human nature, such as the gift of reason or will, which has been added to our nature. Rather, Kaufman writes, "It is . . . man as such, his historical nature, the totality of his being, that is made in God's image."[27] Thus, humans are like God in that, because of their historical nature, they share in the capacity for agency. "Human being, though as dependent on God as other creatures, is an image of God in that it is also a creator."[28] Here we see that for Kaufman what is essential to being human is the capacity for agency—to act as co-creators with God—and it is this understanding of human being that serves as the proper image of God.

"HUMAN BEING" IN KAUFMAN'S *IN FACE OF MYSTERY*

In his book *In Face of Mystery*, Kaufman develops his understanding of human beings as biohistorical—as having the power to create and to understand themselves in and through historical processes.[29] In so doing, he fleshes out the meaning of agency as a capacity fundamental to the human as biohistorical. Kaufman also addresses fully for the first time his contention that symbol use is necessary to this human capacity for agency. He expresses clearly the ways in which agency—at least as Kaufman defines it—requires the ability to negotiate symbols of self and world.

In that book, Kaufman attempts to understand what it means to be human in a way that is respectful of the diversity of ways in which human being has been understood in the history of thought. He seeks an understanding of the human that does not assume its position as the right way or the *standard* in terms of which the human must be understood.[30] To assume such a position is to consider those who deviate from that standard to be less than human; it is to justify discrimination against these individuals. Rather, Kaufman seeks an understanding of human being that can appreciate the diversity of concepts of the human that exist today and throughout human history. To accomplish this task, he reflects on the fact that humans have created diverse understandings of themselves and notes how over time human beings shaped themselves according to the understanding they employed.[31] Thus, Kaufman claims, we human beings are self-creating beings whose identity depends upon our particular understanding of ourselves. We can never understand human being in an immediate way; it can be grasped only reflectively, since it is always shaped by our understanding of ourselves and our relation to ourselves.

Kaufman refers to this human process of self-creating as "historicity," and he understands human beings as fundamentally "historical" beings, able to create themselves as they employ a variety of understandings of themselves over time.[32] This understanding of human being, Kaufman claims, allows us to take seriously the diversity of conceptions of human being without positing the superiority of one view over another. Understanding human beings as those creatures with the capacity to create and shape themselves in a variety of ways, depending upon the conception of human being employed, takes into account the diversity of conceptions of human being.[33] It makes the variety of conceptions of human being an important concern, and thus it is only with some such view, Kaufman claims, that one can avoid a theological anthropology that involves the arbitrary prejudice for one view over another.[34]

Kaufman is well aware that his notion of human beings as historical agents with the capacity for self-creation could imply that human beings exist independently of other forms of life. He is careful to state, "we are related to all other forms of life and through them and with them to inorganic being as well."[35] Were it not for the balances of life, matter, and energy, not only would we cease to exist, but we would never have come into existence in the first place. Thus, Kaufman understands human beings not merely as historical beings, but as biohistorical beings. Human beings are both interdependent upon other forms of life and endowed with the capacity to create themselves and to create culture.[36] Granted, Kaufman claims, it is our historicity that defines us as distinctively human; it is our capacity to transform ourselves and "that ecosystem of life on planet Earth" that makes us distinctively human.[37] But this concept of historicity alone is not adequate for articulating the fundamental assumptions about human nature that Kaufman seeks to address. Rather, Kaufman prefers the term "biohistorical" beings, since it expresses both our nature as self- and culture-creating beings and our interdependence upon other forms of life for our existence and our sustenance.

In an effort to develop his understanding of human beings as biohistorical, Kaufman discusses in detail the "intentional" aspect of the human capacity for creativity, as well as the capacity for symbolization that this intentionality requires. Kaufman defines intentional activity as "setting a goal for ourselves and seeking to attain it."[38] It is an activity that, though it is involved in even the simplest, most mundane of tasks, requires a complex network of mental skills, such as envisioning the options, the decision to act, and the ability to focus attention on the goal of the act. At each point, according to Kaufman, the ability to negotiate a variety of symbols is necessary. First, in order to choose one action among others, we must possess the ability to envision the variety of possible actions. Only once we have imagined the available options is it possible to make a choice for a particular course of action aimed at achieving the desired goal. Such imagination requires the ability to engage symbol in such a way that the possibilities for action are present to our minds. To decide is to choose among a variety of options not yet acted upon; thus, the ability first to symbolize these options is necessary. Second, as the decision is made to act in a particular way, the ability to symbolize retains its importance. As we decide upon an action, it is necessary to keep the intended action in mind in order to guide our acting and to serve as the standard by which we judge the effectiveness of our action. And finally, symbolization is required to focus our attention on the intended goal. It is necessary to retain in our minds the intended goal as we ignore the sensory data that is irrelevant and attend to that which is relevant to accomplishing this goal. The salient point here is that Kaufman's understanding of human being as biohistorical involves the capacity for intentional agency, which requires the ability to symbolize the intended act at every point—in deciding upon an action, guiding the action, and attending to what is significant as we seek to accomplish the intended act. Thus, as our biohistoricity is fundamental to being human, for Kaufman, so too is our capacity for agency and symbolization.[39]

Kaufman's treatment of intentional agency here presupposes an important aspect of human being that has not yet been examined but that is important to my critique of Kaufman's anthropology: the capacity for self-reflexive relations. To act with intention involves the ability to reflect back on oneself. To say or think, "I intend to act this way" is to express in speech one's relatedness with one's self.[40] To say "I" is to refer to oneself, and similarly to say "we" is to refer to the group of which one is a part. Both words are symbolic of self-relatedness and are necessary for the intentional agency to which Kaufman refers. However, it is not only self-relatedness that is required for intentional agency, as Kaufman points out. Agency presupposes not only relatedness to oneself but also relatedness to what is outside the self or community. Agency not only presupposes the "I" or "we" performing the action, but it also requires the object of our intention or the goal of our action that is external to the self. Thus, intentional agency requires the capacity to employ symbols of self and other necessary for relatedness to oneself and relatedness to what is beyond the self.

This capacity for self-reflection is necessary, however, not only with regard to the agent's ability to act, or as Kaufman puts it "to project itself into the future."[41] Furthermore, there are other resources that the agent draws upon in setting a goal and accomplishing that goal than the ability to move ahead-of-itself in action. The agent draws upon experiences *from the past* that open up a variety of options for action, and the agent's past experiences influence the choice of action made. The agent also requires the resource of what Kaufman calls "power": the ability to do things *in the present*, to employ our bodies in purposeful ways to attain the desired goal.[42] What is significant here is that with each resource, the capacity for self-reflection is necessary. The word "I" symbolizes not only the self's relating itself to itself with respect to the future, in the course of action. It also symbolizes the self's relating itself to itself with respect to the past, in the experiences that influence the action, and with respect to the present, in the self's ability to control the body in meaningful ways.[43]

What is problematic here is not so much Kaufman's understanding of intentional agency as requiring the capacity to engage the symbol of self as the self relates to itself and the symbol of other as the self relates to the world. For English speakers, words such as "I" and "we" are what provide us with the symbolic material necessary for the self-consciousness required to act in the world and to accept responsibility for our actions.[44] The problem arises when the capacity for intentional agency, and the requisite capacity for symbolization, becomes privileged as the point at which the nature of human being is located. For Kaufman, this capacity for agency is what distinguishes human beings from animals. While many animals are able to able to act in ways similar to human beings—as when a dog focuses on its particular goal of finding food—their actions are directed by goals that have been set for them by instinct.[45] Human beings, on the other hand, are capable of choosing from a variety of possible actions other than those determined by instinct, and these actions are available to them through symbols that they employ to represent these options to their minds. If we agree with Kaufman that human being is defined by the capacity for agency, including the capacity for symbolization necessary to such agency, then we are left to wonder in what way individuals with profound intellectual disabilities participate in the category human being. This problem with Kaufman's anthropology in *In Face of Mystery* is among the primary reasons I find it in need of revision.

Though I have discussed Kaufman's position that symbolization is crucial for the capacity for agency, it remains to be noted that this position attains even greater force with his claim that agency increases in proportion to the complexity of symbols. This becomes evident in his attempt to demonstrate that it is a mistake to consider agent-selves as coming into existence in isolation from others. One is not born an "I," Kaufman states, "through a more or less autonomous process of growth—like an acorn becoming an oak—in which the full potential present in the seed from the beginning needs only to unfold."[46] Rather, selfhood is attained through participation in a community of persons. It requires socially imposed patterns of behavior and symbolic patterns found initially in interaction between infant and parent and developing further as the self matures to the level of interaction in society.

At each point in the development of a self, interpersonal interaction is required through which the self internalizes social rituals and roles and learns a language.

For Kaufman, as societies with their rituals and roles grow in complexity, so does the possibility for agency. This is because in order for agent-selves to exist there must be enough differentiation to offer a variety of possible choices.[47] As the possible choices of vocation increase, for example, so does the opportunity for individuals to exercise their agency in the process of choosing a vocation.[48] Similarly, for Kaufman, as the level and complexity of symbolization increases, the possibility for agency increases. With very simple languages that include only a few symbolic alternatives, the self is presented with few options for expression, and thus there are fewer options for envisioning an action, for example.[49] As languages grow in complexity, however, a variety of options become available to the individual, and thus the ability to imagine a variety of possibilities for action increases. The point here, for Kaufman, is that language, and the structure of society, are "directly constitutive" of agent-selves.[50] Without adequate complexity of symbolization and social structure, agent-selves would not exist. Because an agent-self is constituted by the language of a particular society, and because human being, as Kaufman understands it, is defined by one's capacity for agency, one is left to wonder the degree to which individuals without language ability, and thus without the capacity for agency, can be considered fully (not deficiently) human given Kaufman's claims.[51]

SUMMARY AND CRITIQUE

In this chapter, I have attempted to accomplish two things: first, to illuminate Kaufman's understanding of human being as possessing capacities for agency and symbolization which he employs in *Systematic Theology* and *In Face of Mystery*, and second, to indicate the variety of ways in which Kaufman privileges the capacities for agency and symbolization. In *Systematic Theology*, Kaufman's treatment of revelation is based on the analogy of personal knowledge, in which the knower remains hidden unless he or she acts with the intent to reveal, and his understanding of the human as agent becomes privileged as that which is essential to human being and as that which properly images the divine. In his *In Face of Mystery*, Kaufman's theological anthropology reaches maturity as he develops his notion of the human as biohistorical agent—as both interdependent on other forms of life and endowed with the capacity to create and understand themselves in and through historical processes. This biohistorical agency requires the capacity to symbolize self and other in order to envision a goal and act to accomplish it. Biohistorical agency and the requisite capacity for symbolization become privileged as the point at which the nature of human being is located.

The capacity for agency is privileged in Kaufman's theological anthropology as an expression of that which is essential to human being. The capacity for purposeful agency and the accompanying capacity for the negotiation of symbols of self and world are considered necessary to human being as that which distinguishes human being from the rest of creation. As Kaufman states in *Systematic Theology*, humanity's historicity is more than an attribute or feature of human nature; it is "the totality of his being."[52] And in *In Face of Mystery*, Kaufman states that the capacity for agency is the very quality that distinguishes human beings from animals.[53] He considers language to be "directly constitutive of agent-selves."[54]

My position in response to Kaufman here is that his understanding of human being as inherently historical, with capacities for purposive agency and symbolization, fails to meet the very requirements that he established for defining what counts as an adequate religious symbol, which he describes as "appropriateness to the broad spectrum of human experience and thus provides an understanding of human life that is meaningful."[55] It cannot serve as an understanding that gives meaning to the lives of individuals with profound intellectual disabilities, because it cannot take into account their inability to act purposively. Many such individuals do not possess the motor skills to employ their body in ways that are capable of accomplishing a goal. But it also does not take into account that many of these individuals do not possess capacities for self-reflection and symbolization necessary to envision a goal and intend to accomplish it. This requires the intellectual capacity to negotiate concepts of self and other that many individuals with profound intellectual disabilities do not possess. What meaning could Kaufman's understanding of human being as inherently possessing the capacities for purposive agency and symbolization confer to individuals with profound intellectual disabilities, except that they are somehow deficient human beings? Kaufman's understanding of human being cannot fulfill his own requirement of adequacy for religious symbols because it lacks the comprehensiveness that takes into account the situation of the individuals with profound intellectual disabilities, and thus I find it is a concept in need of reconstruction.

There is a further privileging of the agential self in Kaufman's theological anthropology as it becomes the proper image of the divine. In *Systematic Theology*, Kaufman defines the *imago Dei* in terms of humanity's historicity: that human beings are both being made by history and creating and furthering history. Humans are like God in that, because of their historical nature, they share in the capacity for agency.[56] One is left to wonder at this point in what way individuals with intellectual disabilities are able to properly image the divine, since they are not endowed with this privileged capacity for purposeful agency. It seems safe to assume that, given Kaufman's understanding of the term, the *imago Dei* is not present in these individuals.

By failing to take into account the situation of the individuals with profound intellectual disabilities—through privileging the agential, symbolizing self as the location of that which is essential to human being and as that which properly images the divine—Kaufman's anthropology falls short of his own criterion for adequate religious symbols, appropriateness to a broad spectrum of human experiences, enough to be meaningful for human life. Thus, I claim, Kaufman's concept of the human as agent requires reconstruction. Following Kaufman's lead, I broaden the range of human situations considered in the development of a theological anthropology, in an effort "to root out one-sidedness, prejudice and bias."[57] Given adequate attention to the situation of individuals with profound intellectual disabilities as unable to participate in language use, symbolization, or intentional agency, I will argue that a more helpful, less discriminatory conception of human being can be constructed. With the help of Martin Buber's dialogical thought, I will argue that human being is located in the sphere of "the between."[58] It is not located in an intellectual capacity possessed by the individual, but rather it is located in I-Thou relationships in which there is the mutual responsiveness of one to another.[59] Following Buber's thought, I will argue that it is only through these relationships of mutual responsiveness that relationship with God can be truly realized.[60] Thus, for Buber, the sphere of "the between" is not only the location of our humanity; it is also the location of the experience of God.[61] To conceive of human being in this way is to avoid dependence on the capacities for agency, symbolization, and language use available only to those with adequate intellectual skills. It is a way to conceive of human being that is open to those with profound intellectual disabilities, and thus it is a conception of human being that should be taken more seriously in the Christian theological community.

This revision of the concept of the human need not mean that intentionality, symbolization, linguisticality, and agency are no longer honored as valuable to human life. I do not intend to leave these capacities behind. I do not deny that the capacity to engage symbols of self and other allow an individual to act with purpose, for good and for ill. I do not deny that human relationships of mutual love and responsiveness gain a level of depth and devotion through verbal and intellectual interaction. What I am contesting here is the tendency in Kaufman's theology, and in much of Western thought, to privilege the capacity for language use as that which distinguishes human beings vis-à-vis other living beings. What is wrong here is not the affirmation of linguisticality, symbolization, and agency, but the privileging of these capacities as the absolute quality that defines human being. Through engaging the dialogical philosophy of Martin Buber, I hope to broaden the traditional understanding of human being in Christian theology, in a way that acknowledges the full humanity of individuals with profound intellectual disabilities. Though these individuals do not possess intellectual and linguistic capacities to act with purpose or to participate in relationships of intellectual depth and complexity, they do participate in relationships of mutual responsiveness. They are responsive to the world around them. They respond to pain, to the presence of another, to contrasts in color, to the sound of music in the background. Though this capacity for responsiveness does not afford relationships of great complexity, it does allow the possibility for relationships of mutual responsiveness. With the help of Martin Buber, it is in these relationships, I will argue, that our humanity is located.

I do not intend to be fully historicist in my reconstruction of the concept of human being. There is a sense in which I am making an essentialist move in my efforts to locate human being in relationships of mutual responsiveness, though the essentialism I employ is not an absolute one. Rather, returning to our earlier treatment of essentialism, it is of the "strategic" variety. I find it necessary to recommend an alternative for speaking of human being in an effort to acknowledge the full humanity of individuals with profound intellectual disabilities, as well as to acknowledge the ways in which the concept of the human has traditionally been discriminatory against them. My essentialist reconstruction is "strategic" in this sense. However, I am also acutely aware, with Kaufman, that I am unable to gain direct access to reality, including the nature of human being. Thus, my efforts to speak of human being in a way that is mindful of the dignity and humanity of the intellectually disabled is historicist in the sense that it is always open to change and critique given the input of others whose insights are inaccessible to me.

2. George Lindbeck: Human Being as Language User

UNLIKE GORDON KAUFMAN, whose theological anthropology is developed thoroughly and explicitly, George Lindbeck does not develop a full fledged theological anthropology in the course of his writings. His major work, *The Nature of Doctrine: Religion and Theology in a Postliberal Age*, addresses primarily epistemological and methodological issues, not anthropological ones. In particular, it is a response to the question of how to conceive of religious doctrines in a way that resolves doctrinal conflict without resort to the capitulation of one doctrine to another.[1] He seeks to understand how theologians of diverse traditions can claim to have reconciled their once-conflicting theological positions without requiring that one or the other party abandon his or her position, and he seeks to understand such claims without denying their legitimacy by speculating that the participants in the dialogue are victims of their own desire for reconciliation. The problem, according to Lindbeck, is not with the legitimacy of the claims to reconciliation. Rather, the problem is with the inadequacy of the ways in which doctrines and religion have been conceived. Thus, Lindbeck's work is an attempt to provide an understanding of doctrine and religion, which he calls the "rule theory of doctrine" and the "cultural-linguistic theory of religion," in a way that explains the possibility of this doctrinal "reconciliation without capitulation" without denying its legitimacy.[2] It is not an attempt to provide an understanding of human being.

Despite Lindbeck's epistemological focus in *The Nature of Doctrine*, as with any epistemology there is an anthropology that is assumed. And although his anthropological assumptions remain primarily implicit, there are times in which his assumptions are revealed in a more direct way, though always with the aim of bolstering his theories

of religion and doctrine. In this chapter, I will discuss the anthropological assumptions of Lindbeck's theory of religion and the
implications of his anthropology for individuals with profound
intellectual disabilities for whom language use is not an option. While
Lindbeck may find his cultural-linguistic theory of religion
better suited to address the problem of doctrinal reconciliation without
capitulation, his theory assumes that to be human requires the ability
to negotiate linguistic material and that to participate in experience of
any kind one must have the capacity to negotiate symbols. Such an
assumption leads to the unhappy conclusion that individuals without
the ability to negotiate linguistic material are deficiently human.

THE CULTURAL-LINGUISTIC THEORY OF RELIGION

To demonstrate the usefulness of the cultural-linguistic approach
to religion for understanding doctrinal reconciliation without capitulation, Lindbeck compares his theory of religion to other regnant
theories, which he claims fail at this task. One is the propositionalist
theory, in which religion is conceived as similar to science or philosophy, with its emphasis on the cognitive meaningfulness of religious
utterances. Here doctrines are useful as "informative propositions or
truth claims about objective realities." Another is what Lindbeck calls
the "experiential-expressive" theory of religion, which emphasizes
the inner, experiential aspect of the religious life. Here doctrines are
conceived as "noninformative and nondiscursive symbols of inner
feelings, attitudes, or existential orientations."[3]

According to Lindbeck, both theories of religion, and their accompanying theories of doctrine, fail to adequately explain the ways in
which theologians claim to have come to some agreement over once
divisive theological positions without either side abandoning their
position. For the propositionalist view of religion, the meaning of doctrines is found in their truth-value. Once a doctrine is true, it is always
true. As a result, reconciliation of two disparate theological positions is
not possible unless one theological position is abandoned in exchange
for the other. In the case of experiential expressivism, the meaning
of doctrines is based on the religiously significant feelings that they

symbolize. Thus, religious reconciliation or conflict is based on simi-
larity or difference in experiences, not doctrinal consistency or change.
Faithfulness to a particular doctrinal formulation is irrelevant here, as
long as it is expressive of the shared religious experience. Similarly, the
capitulation of one doctrine for another is not a problem as long as
there is harmony in underlying religious feelings.[4]

Given the limits of the available theories of religion and doctrine,
Lindbeck proposes an alternative that he finds better able to explain
doctrinal reconciliation without recapitulation: a "cultural-linguistic"
approach to religion and a "regulative" or "rule" theory of doctrine.
This theory of religion has appeared in various areas of study,
including anthropology, sociology, and psychology. But, according
to Lindbeck, it has not been accepted by the majority of scholars
of theology and religion for a variety of reasons.[5] Here religion is
conceived neither as similar to science with its emphasis on the
cognitive meaningfulness of religious statements nor as expressive of
shared religious experiences. Rather, religion is conceived as similar to
culture, understood using Clifford Geertz's definition as a set of
control mechanisms—symbolic rules in the form of words, gestures,
objects, and so on—for the governing of behavior.[6] Thus, Lindbeck
defines religion as "a kind of cultural and/or linguistic framework or
medium that shapes the entirety of life and thought."[7] Given this view
of religion, doctrines are conceived neither as propositional statements
of truth nor as symbolic statements expressive of an underlying
religious sentiment. Rather, doctrines function here as "communally
authoritative rules of discourse, attitude, and action."[8]

As Lindbeck sees it, to consider doctrines in this way allows us to
explain the possibility of reconciling two very different doctrines
without the capitulation of one to the other. To use his example, the
rules "Drive on the left" and "Drive on the right" clearly oppose one
another, and they retain their meaning regardless of the circumstances
at hand. However, under different circumstances both rules may be
binding—say, one when traffic is normal and the other when an
accident is to be avoided. Opposition between rules, or doctrines in
this case, may be resolved not by changing one or the other, but simply
by specifying the context in which the rule or doctrine applies. Thus,
for Lindbeck, to conceive of doctrines as rules versus truth claims or

expressive symbols provides a coherent way to conceive of doctrinal reconciliation without capitulation.

Despite the usefulness of the cultural-linguistic theory of religion and the rule theory of doctrine for dealing with doctrinal conflict, Lindbeck finds that this approach requires considerable defense to promote its adoption among theologians and religiously interested scholars of religion, especially given the competing influence of the experiential-expressive approach.[9] To build such a defense, Lindbeck attempts to demonstrate the superiority of the cultural-linguistic approach to religion for dealing with both nontheological and theological concerns. It is here that the anthropological assumptions of Lindbeck's theory become clear.

ON THE SUPERIORITY OF THE CULTURAL-LINGUISTIC THEORY OF RELIGION

The particular nontheological concern that Lindbeck addresses is the relationship between religion and experience. He argues that the cultural-linguistic approach to religion is better able to handle the anthropological data involved in the examination of this relationship than the experiential-expressive approach. He develops his argument primarily with a comparison of the two approaches and asks whether it is conceptually better to think of religions as expressive products of those experiences of the divine that are often described as "religious" or as producers of experience.[10]

Lindbeck describes the experiential-expressive theory of religion with reference to one of its major representatives, the well-known Roman Catholic theologian Bernard Lonergan. In *Method in Theology*, Lonergan provides six theses of his theory of religion, which Lindbeck takes to be characteristic of experiential-expressivism.[11] Lindbeck summarizes them as follows:

1. Different religions are diverse expressions of a common core experience.
2. The experience, while conscious, may be unknown on the level of self-conscious reflection.

3. It is present in all human beings.

4. In most religions, experience is the source and norm of objectifications.

5. The primordial religious experience is characterized as "the dynamic state of being in love without restrictions" or "God's gift of love,"[12] which Lindbeck likens to Tillich's notion of being grasped by ultimate concern.[13]

6. The objectivities of biblical religions are not simply the expressive symbols of religious experience but have their source in God's "revelatory will."[14]

What is most significant for Lindbeck's comparative purposes is Lonergan's claim, which he shares with other experiential expressivists, that the variety of religions is expressive of a common core experience.

In Lindbeck's discussion of the cultural-linguistic approach to religion, he defines religion as "comprehensive interpretive schemes, usually embodied in myths or narratives and heavily ritualized, which structure human experience and understanding of self and world."[15] Religion is not a set of truth claims, nor does it function as symbols expressive of inner feelings or experiences. Rather, religion is like a cultural or linguistic system that shapes all aspects of human life. Like a language or culture, Lindbeck claims, religion is a communal phenomenon that shapes the experiences of individuals rather than primarily being shaped by them. With each aspect of Lindbeck's description of the cultural-linguistic approach to religion, what is significant to note is the consistent expression that religions are not derivative of human experience, but producers of experience.[16]

Thus, in regard to the relationship between religion and experience, the experiential-expressive approach emphasizes the ways in which religion is an expressive product of experience, while the cultural-linguistic approach emphasizes the converse, that religion is the producer of experience. It is too simplistic, Lindbeck avers, to conceive of this relationship as unidirectional. With the cultural-linguistic approach, it is not the case that religions remain unaffected by experience and serve only as its producer. Rather, the relationship is a dialectical one. Religion both affects and is affected by experience.

Even so, Lindbeck claims, within his cultural-linguistic approach to religion the "external" religious factors take the lead in the interplay with the "internal" experiential ones.[17]

The cultural-linguistic approach emphasizes the ways in which experience is never prelinguistic but is always shaped and even constituted by cultural and linguistic forms. Lindbeck uses the example of the young Helen Keller and so-called wolf children to illustrate his point. These are cases of individuals who, without language ability, were unable to actualize their human capacities for thought, action, and feeling. So, too, in the case of the relationship between religion and experience, in order to participate in religious experience one must have the capacity to comprehend the linguistic system of a particular religion. As Lindbeck writes, "To become a Christian involves learning the story of Israel and Jesus well enough to interpret and experience oneself and one's world in its terms."[18]

It is in Lindbeck's efforts to defend the superiority of this cultural-linguistic approach to religion at explaining the relationship between religion and experience that his discriminatory anthropology becomes clear. This is because his efforts involve the claim that experience of any kind, religious or otherwise, is not possible without the capacity to negotiate the symbolic structure of language. This is the case, Lindbeck states, because experience is not possible without the means to express it. At first glance this statement seems unproblematic, as it could be inclusive of a variety of means of expression, not only those that are symbolic. He later clarifies, however, that the means for expression necessary for experience are "signs and symbols." To experience something requires the ability to recognize an experience as experience—to identify it as such—which in turn requires the ability to negotiate signs and symbols. Thus, according to Lindbeck, "the richer our expressive or linguistic system the more subtle, varied, and differentiated can be our experience."[19]

While it may be the case that as one's capacity to employ complex symbol systems grows one is open to a greater variety of experiences, Lindbeck has gone too far in his claim that the ability to negotiate sign and symbol is necessary for the participation in experience of any kind. And while it may be the case that the means for expressing an experience is necessary in order to have it, there are a variety of means for expression that are not symbolic. I am thinking in particular here of individuals with profound intellectual disabilities who do not have the capacity to employ symbolic material, but who still express themselves in a variety of ways through body motion, sound, changes in body temperature and behavioral state, and the like.[20] To conceive of "the means of expression" more broadly to include nonsymbolic means is to open up the concept of experience to include those unable to employ symbolic material as a means to express it. To employ Lindbeck's conception of experience as requiring the ability to negotiate sign and symbol, however, is to exclude individuals with profound intellectual disabilities from among the privileged group of experiencing beings. And, to the degree that participation in experience is necessary to being human, Lindbeck's limited view of experience leads to the conclusion that those who are unable to participate in this linguistically mediated experience are deficiently human. It is to conclude that linguistic ability is necessary to being human, and therefore those without this ability are human in a deficient way. Thus, I find that the conception of human being Lindbeck assumes in the defense of his cultural-linguistic approach to religion is discriminatory toward individuals with profound intellectual disabilities and is in need of reconstruction.

ON THE MEANING OF PRIVATE LANGUAGE AND EXPERIENCE IN WITTGENSTEIN

To defend his case for the superiority of the cultural-linguistic approach to religion over the experiential-expressive approach, Lindbeck turns to the thought of Ludwig Wittgenstein for support. Lindbeck claims that Wittgenstein argues, as he does, that there is no way in which language is an unmediated expression of private human experience: "All symbol systems have their origin in interpersonal relations and social interactions."[21] This argument can be found, Lindbeck states, in Wittgenstein's claim that private languages are logically impossible. If Lindbeck and Wittgenstein (as Lindbeck reads him) are right, then according to Lindbeck it is equally impossible to have experiences that are purely private, since experience (as Lindbeck conceives it) requires symbolization, and symbolization is never private.

As I see it, however, Lindbeck has misinterpreted Wittgenstein's argument regarding the privacy of language and experience. Yes, Wittgenstein resists the word "private" as a descriptor of language or experience, but it is in a sense very different from the one Lindbeck uses. In fact, Wittgenstein's thought on this subject provides support for the very position that Lindbeck sets out to resist—that language is not a necessary condition for experience but rather is often dependent on primitive, prelinguistic, instinctive human responses.[22]

To clarify the way in which Lindbeck has misunderstood Wittgenstein's rejection of private languages and experiences, it will be helpful to turn to Wittgenstein's famous "beetle-in-a-box" thought experiment. Here Wittgenstein clarifies the sense in which he denies the descriptor "private" to name language or experience. In this passage, Wittgenstein argues that it is erroneous to conceive of our words as private and expressive of objects that only the speaker can know. As an analogy, he considers the possibility that everyone had a box with something in it that he or she each named a "beetle." The participants stated that they knew what a "beetle" was only by looking in their own boxes and that they had no access to the box of another. Wittgenstein then asks, "Suppose the word 'beetle' had a use in these people's language?"[23] If so, he states, then what is in the box is irrelevant. The word "beetle" could not be used to name a thing, that is, an insect, or as Wittgenstein puts it, "a something," since the box could be empty in each case, or each person could have something different in the box. The important point here is that our words do not refer to something private and inaccessible to others. Our words find meaning in their use. It is language that establishes the meaning of a thing, in which case our words cannot refer to something purely private and inaccessible to others. In Wittgenstein's words, "grammar tells us what kind of object anything is."[24]

Wittgenstein uses this passage to demonstrate that to assume that our words are expressive of sense objects only the speaker can know is in effect to make the sensation irrelevant, "not even as a something,"[25] since what these words refer to may vary with each person who uses them. Such a view of language and sensation is faulty, according to

Wittgenstein, because it is based on an inadequate view of the human person. It is based on a dualistic view of the human person in which sensations are taken to be private, as "a something," in the sense that they are objects of "inner" perception possessing essential characteristics apart from a living organism, while the body is considered to be senseless and "exterior" to the sensing mind. In fact, however, to assume that our words reflect sensations or experiences that are utterly private is to make them irrelevant to the language game.[26]

It is not the case, however, that for Wittgenstein there is no sense in which a sensation can be "private." He expresses this in the statement, "It is not a something, but not a nothing either!"[27] Rather than view the human person in a dualistic sense in which the body is taken to be senseless and sensations are taken to be objects of "inner" perception accessible only to the perceiving person, Wittgenstein maintains a monist view in which sensations are taken to be states of a living organism that have natural expression in the behavior of living organisms. Thus, sensations, for Wittgenstein, are not a "something," purely private objects of "inner" perception accessible only to the perceiving person, in the sense that a dualist would take them.[28] But sensations are also not a "nothing." They are not irrelevant to the language game because they find their natural expression in the behavior of the living organism, and that behavior includes language.[29] In this sense we can say that, for Wittgenstein, sensations may be private, because they remain sensations of individual living organisms. However, insofar as these sensations find expression in the behavior of living beings—and because behavior is a bodily phenomenon, it is always public—they are not private and are fully accessible to the observer.

How, then, has Lindbeck misused Wittgenstein to bolster his position that the cultural-linguistic approach to religion is superior to the experiential-expressivist approach at handling nontheological data? Lindbeck's thesis with regard to the relationship between religion and experience is that experience does not produce religion, but rather that religion produces experience. Experience is never prelinguistic but is always shaped and even constituted by cultural and linguistic forms. To support this thesis, he claims that it is conceptually confused to speak of experiences that are private, and he turns to Wittgenstein, stating that both he and Wittgenstein reject private experiences and share a similar use of the word "private." Having clarified the sense in which Wittgenstein rejects experiences as "private," we can begin to see how Lindbeck has misread him.

Lindbeck rejects the notion of private experience in a sense very different from that of Wittgenstein. For Lindbeck, the descriptor "private" names the origination of experience as prelinguistic. It names experience as that which is not "in some fashion symbolized."[30] To name an experience "private" means, for Lindbeck, that it does not require language, "or, more generally, some conceptual and/or symbolic interpretive scheme," as a condition for its existence.[31] Clearly, Lindbeck rejects this understanding of experience as contradictory to the claim he sets out to defend—that language is a condition for experience.

As we have seen, Wittgenstein's use of the word "private" with regard to experience takes on a very different meaning. In fact, the sense in which he rejects experience as "private" serves as a challenge to Lindbeck's very claim that language is a necessary condition for experience. Wittgenstein rejects the notion of private experience only in the sense that a dualist would view them, as "inner" objects accessible only to the perceiving individual, with no connection to their expression in "outer" human behavior. We have seen that Wittgenstein rejects this perspective in favor of a monist one in which sensations are considered to have natural expression in the behavior of living organism. Lindbeck has wrongly turned to Wittgenstein in support of his claim that it is conceptually confused to speak of experiences that are purely private, since, for Wittgenstein, the notion of "private" with regard to experience has nothing to do with whether or not experience originated in language. It has to do, rather, with experiences, or "sensations," and their relationship with bodily behavior, including language.[32]

It is at this point that we begin to see the ways in which Wittgenstein's thoughts on experience actually challenge rather than support Lindbeck's most basic claims. In keeping with his perspective of the human person as a living organism with sensations and experiences that find their natural expression in behavior, Wittgenstein claims that language itself is just one form of behavior that serves to express our bodily sensations and experiences. And even further, contrary to Lindbeck's claim that language is a necessary condition for experience, Wittgenstein expresses in numerous ways and in numerous instances that certain primitive, instinctive human responses are necessary for language games to arise.[33] He expresses this mostly clearly in *Zettel* when he addresses the question of what it means to say that we know another is in pain. We do infer that someone is in pain based on his or her behavior, but according to Wittgenstein, it is not an inference based on analogy from our own experience of expressing similar behavior when we are in pain. Rather, the inference is a primitive reaction. He writes, "It is a help here to remember that it is a primitive reaction to tend, to treat, the part that hurts when someone else is in pain." In keeping with Wittgenstein's monist perspective of the human person, bodily behavior is significant as expressive of sensations or, in this case, the sensation of pain. The fact that the individual is in pain is not inaccessible to the observer. What is significant here is that, for Wittgenstein, the inference of the observer that the individual is in pain is a primitive response to the behavior of the individual that is prelinguistic.[34] Knowing someone is in pain, doubting someone is in pain, and so forth are prelinguistic, natural, instinctive behaviors toward others of which language is merely an extension. Wittgenstein expresses this most explicitly when he writes, "But what is the word 'primitive' meant to say here? Presumably that this sort of behavior is *pre-linguistic*: that a language-game is based *on it*, that it is the prototype of a way of thinking and not a result of thought."[35] We can see clearly here that it is not the case that Wittgenstein supports the notion that language is necessary for experience, as Lindbeck claims he does, but rather that Wittgenstein acknowledges ways in which the converse is true—that our language is often dependent upon primitive, prelinguistic expressions of our experiences.

Wittgenstein advances this same perspective in *Philosophical Investigations*. He continues his penchant for problematizing the notion of "private" language and asks, "How do words *refer* to sensations?" Wittgenstein rejects again the notion of private language when it comes to sensations, insofar as by "private" we mean sensations that are "inner" and accessible only to the perceiving individual, and he responds with a similar statement to the one found in *Zettel*: "Here is one possibility: words are connected with the primitive, the natural, expressions of the sensation and used in their place."[36] He uses the word "pain" as an example again and suggests that when a child hurts himself and cries, this is a primitive, natural expression of the pain sensation. It follows from here that adults teach him new pain behavior in the form of words and sentences. In contrast to Lindbeck, pain language in this case is not primary. It is not necessary that the child acquire the ability to use the word "pain" in order to have the painful experience or even in order to express the painful sensation, but rather pain language is derivative of primitive, prelinguistic expressions of the painful sensation.

The compelling question here becomes this: Why has Lindbeck misread Wittgenstein? Why has Lindbeck misinterpreted Wittgenstein's use of the word "private" with regard to language and experience in an effort to bolster his support for a cultural-linguistic approach to religion? Perhaps Lindbeck has misinterpreted the sense in which Wittgenstein rejects private experience because to interpret him rightly would be to contradict the very argument he sets out to defend. If, as Wittgenstein suggests, sensations are states of a living organism that find their natural expression in the behavior of that living organism and are not merely objects of "inner" perception available only to the perceiving individual, and if language is one form of this behavior that is expressive of these sensations, then it is not the case, as Lindbeck claims, that language is necessary for experience. In fact, as we have noted, Wittgenstein argues that the converse is the case: Language is based on primitive, prelinguistic expressions of sensations. To read Wittgenstein rightly with regard to his rejection of private experience, Lindbeck would have to surrender the very claim he sets out to support: that language is a necessary condition for experience.

Even further, perhaps Lindbeck is unable to interpret Wittgenstein rightly because Lindbeck assumes the very position regarding private experience that Wittgenstein rejects. This seems evident from the ways in which Lindbeck speaks of religious experience. He uses a variety of spatial metaphors to speak of religious experience such as "deep" and "inner."[37] He does this not only in his efforts to describe the experiential-expressivist position, but also to describe his own cultural-linguistic approach to religion as "the interplay between 'inner' experience and the 'external' religious and cultural factors," with the latter viewed as leading partners in this interplay.[38] This suggests that Lindbeck is working with the notion of experience as objects of "inner" perception that are available only to the perceiving individual. It is ironic that Lindbeck has turned to the thought of Wittgenstein to bolster his argument for the superiority of a cultural-linguistic approach to religion when, in the end, Wittgenstein serves to challenge Lindbeck's primary claim and one of his most basic assumptions.

Despite the limitations of Lindbeck's treatment of the relationship between language and experience, it is not the case that Lindbeck's cultural-linguistic approach to religion is without its salutary aspects. Lindbeck's efforts to defend the claim that religious culture and language influence human experience are valuable and are not contested here. What is contestable, however, is that in the process of defending this claim, Lindbeck takes things too far and, in the end, disregards the ways in which experience is not dependent upon language. Yes, cultural and linguistic factors influence experience, but there is a dialectic here that requires further attention. Lindbeck initially acknowledges the dialectical character of this interaction but later neglects it, particularly when he claims that experience is not possible without symbolization. Lindbeck turns to Wittgenstein for support of this claim, but as I have shown, Lindbeck has misinterpreted Wittgenstein, who attends to that aspect of the dialectic that Lindbeck neglects: the ways in which experience is not necessarily dependent upon symbolization but rather is often the prelinguistic precursor to it.

Wittgenstein's own approach to the relationship of language and experience not only helpfully dispatches Lindbeck's position; it also offers a more adequate anthropology than the one Lindbeck employs. For Wittgenstein, human being is not defined by the ability to express oneself with sign and symbol. Rather, human being is thought of as a living, sensing being whose expression of these sensations flows naturally in the form of a variety of behaviors, language being only one of them. For Wittgenstein, words, then, function not to form our experiences but to express them; our words "are tied up with the natural expression of sensations."[39] Rather than limiting human being to the ability to participate in language, Wittgenstein suggests that we understand human being more as a living being who possesses a variety of means for self-expression. Thus, in contrast to Lindbeck, Wittgenstein opens up the concept of human being to include those who are unable to express themselves symbolically.

In the end, I am not optimistic about cultural-linguistic approaches to religion as a methodology for doing theology with the concerns of individuals with profound intellectual disabilities in mind. The determined commitment to the "story" and "grammar" of the Christian tradition seems to lead inevitably to problems of discrimination when these individuals are taken into account. In Lindbeck's case, in what way could individuals with a profound intellectual disability be considered human in a nondeficient way, given his claim that experience is not possible without the capacity to negotiate the symbolic structure of language?

THE LIMITS OF A STORY-BOUND THEOLOGY

The problems with Lindbeck's cultural-linguistic approach to religion vis-à-vis individuals with profound intellectual disabilities are not unique to him. His firm commitment to the story of the Christian tradition proves problematic for others with cultural-linguistic affinities. The work of the Christian theologian and ethicist Stanley Hauerwas is a case in point. Though he has written extensively over a number of years on behalf of individuals with profound intellectual disabilities, his cultural-linguistic loyalties to the Christian story in fact raise problems when these individuals are taken into account.

Hauerwas consistently emphasizes the distinction between the Christian church and the world, which results from the loyalty of Christians to the story of their faith. He writes, "The church is the place where the story of God is enacted, told, and heard."[40] The world, by contrast, "is not a community and has no such story."[41] Christians are those who have chosen to believe that Jesus is Lord; the people of the world are those who have taken the freedom not yet to believe.[42] For Hauerwas, it is important that Christians emphasize the particularity of the narrative that "makes us what we are in the first place."[43] The Christian story is what gives Christians their definition, their uniqueness. To be Christian, Hauerwas claims, is to affirm oneself as having found one's destiny only through locating oneself within the story of God. This means that truth cannot be known—Jesus cannot be known—until one has been changed by the story of Jesus Christ, and this transformation takes place, according to Hauerwas, as one hears the story and chooses to believe it.[44]

As I read Hauerwas here, particularly with individuals with profound intellectual disabilities in mind, the question of where these individuals fit in this schema of story-bound Christians and storyless people of the world seems obvious. It is ironic that in the work of a scholar dedicated to individuals with profound intellectual disabilities, these individuals appear relegated to the status of the invisible and the undefined. Individuals with profound intellectual disabilities are not only unable to comprehend the Christian story, but they are also unable to make a conscious choice of either faithfulness or unfaithfulness to it. As a result, given Hauerwas's distinction between those who learn and choose to accept the Christian story and those who do not, individuals with profound intellectual disabilities belong neither to the community of believers nor to the community-less population of the worldly. Rather, they do not appear to exist at all as a population worth distinction.

Hauerwas appears to anticipate this difficulty when he employs language like "the gestures of a truthful story" versus emphasizing the words of the story. He states it is not only through words that we learn the story. We learn the story not only by hearing but also by acting out the story. For example, as Hauerwas sees it, we learn to pray only by first knowing how to kneel. He finds that this emphasis upon learning the story through gestures versus words assists us in including individuals with profound intellectual disabilities among those who learn the Christian story. In fact, he states, these individuals serve as a test case for the possibility of knowing the Christian story through gestures.[45] As I see it, though, the fact remains that, for Hauerwas, the gestures serve the story, and not the other way around. "We must be taught the gestures that help position our bodies and our souls to be able to rightly hear and then retell the story."[46] The aim of Hauerwas's distinction between the church and the world is to emphasize the importance of faithfulness to the Christian story, which defines our uniqueness as Christians; his aim is not to affirm faithfulness to particular gestures. Leaving aside the question of whether individuals with profound intellectual disabilities will be physically able to participate in these story-learning gestures,[47] Hauerwas's dependence on the story, on hearing and retelling it, and on recognizing and responding to its saintly practitioners makes one wonder whether his theology is really directed at serving individuals with profound intellectual disabilities, or whether he engages individuals with profound intellectual disabilities to serve his story-bound theology.

Given such difficulties with cultural-linguistic approaches to religion, I find more possibility for the kind of theology that respects the dignity and humanity of individuals with profound intellectual disabilities in approaches that, like Kaufman's, are more thoroughly historicist in nature. While the emphasis on purposive agency and symbolization in Kaufman's anthropology is clearly limited vis-à-vis individuals with profound intellectual disabilities, the historicist methodology that he employs leaves open the possibility of revision of his anthropology, given the current growing awareness of individuals with profound intellectual disabilities as a population requiring our attention. The emphasis of historicism on the particular and the concrete reminds us that theology is not the search for an unchanging grammar or story in religious traditions. Rather, it involves an appreciation of all religious claims as localized, relative to time and place, and infused by the interests of those who make such claims.[48] With a historicist methodology, our religious claims are always open to change, given attention to the voices of the marginalized. As a result, I find it inherently better as a guide for theologians in their efforts to do theology in a way that is mindful of individuals with profound intellectual disabilities among us.

Lindbeck's cultural-linguistic approach to religion is arguably also historicist in nature.[49] His emphasis on the particularity of all claims to knowledge, including his emphasis on the cultural and linguistic nature of human experience, does indicate his historicist tendencies. However, Lindbeck's emphasis on the grammar or story of the Christian religion as unchanging and the demand of faithfulness to it give the impression that religions are "disembodied" and free from the influence of social, political, economic, and kindred factors.[50] As I have attempted to argue in this chapter, adequate attention to individuals with profound intellectual disabilities renders problematic Lindbeck's emphasis on the linguistic nature of all human experience and the accompanying conception of human being as inherently linguistic, since such emphases assume the deficiency of individuals without capacities for language use.

3. Human Being in Relational Terms: A Phenomenology

AS AN ALTERNATIVE to defining human beings as creatures who possess the capacity for conceptualization, in the next two chapters I claim that human being is better understood in relational terms, as participation in relationships of mutual responsiveness. This anthropology locates human being not in some capacity possessed by an individual, whether that is the ability for conceptualization, the freedom to choose, or upright stature. Human being is not defined by some capacity located in the individual in isolation from the world around her. Rather, human being is considered here as participation in the meeting between responsive partners. Granted that such participation requires the capacity to respond, this capacity alone is not sufficient for understanding human being as I see it, for mutual responsiveness requires a partner who responds to us and to whom one responds.

This alternative anthropology is significant for my purposes, since it is broad enough to accord full humanity to individuals with profound intellectual disabilities for whom relationships of mutual responsiveness are a possibility, while the capacity for conceptualization is not.[1] To demonstrate my point, in this chapter I give a phenomenological description of the responsive relations of an individual with a profound intellectual disability. This individual, whom I name Chan, is constructed based on my experience of relationship with individuals with profound intellectual disabilities, accumulated over the years of my clinical practice as a physical therapist. This phenomenological description will show that Chan does not possess the capacity to employ concepts of self and other required for intentional agency—a capacity central to Kaufman's understanding of what it means to be human. Similarly, his behavior does not reflect an ability to express himself symbolically using public gestures, words, or actions with the intent to give meaning to experience—an ability that Lindbeck considers central to defining what it means to be human.[2] However, as the case study will show, Chan is an individual who does participate in responsive relations with his caregivers and friends, and it is this participation in mutually responsive relations that is expressive of what it means to be human.

As a resource for my interpretation of the responsive relations of Chan as expressive of his full humanity, I turn in the next chapter to the dialogical philosophy of Martin Buber. Although Buber does not elaborate on the significance of his philosophy for understanding the full humanity of such individuals, I find his thought especially helpful, since for Buber human being is a dialogical concept. To be human, for Buber, is not to possess a particular capacity but rather to meet the other in a relationship of mutual responsiveness, totalization, and immediacy.[3] Such meeting takes place not on one or the other side of the subject/object dichotomy, but in the realm of "the between"—"the other side of the subjective, this side of the objective, on the narrow ridge at which I and Thou meet one another."[4] There is no place for conceptualization here, since conceptualization involves a departure from the immediacy of the relation as one categorizes, compares, and evaluates particular aspects of the other. Rather, when I and Thou meet, they engage in the sheer presence of the other, aware of the other as Thou and freed from the objectification of the other through a reflective effort to evaluate and categorize. Buber's efforts here to conceive of human being in terms of the aspect of human relationships that is free from rationalization and conceptualization, rather than in terms of the possession of a particular capacity, I find are helpful in understanding the relationality of individuals with profound intellectual disabilities and thus their humanity.

A FRAMEWORK FOR COMMUNICATION

Before I begin a phenomenological description of the relationality of Chan, let me first offer a theoretical framework to describe the developmental process of the emergence of communication and language. This framework will provide concepts that are helpful in identifying the level of communication and intentionality of individuals like Chan. Ellen Siegel and Amy Wetherby employ a three-staged model for understanding the development of communication and language.[5] From birth to about nine months of age, the infant is in the perlocutionary (preintentional) stage in which his or her behavior affects the caregiver, and thus serves a communicative function. There is no employment of signals with the intent to accomplish a particular goal at this stage of communication, and there is no realization that his or her behavior can affect others.[6] At about nine months of age, the infant demonstrates the ability to use preverbal gestures with the intent to communicate. The infant uses signals to communicate with the intent to accomplish a preplanned goal. This is the illocutionary (intentional preverbal) stage. At about thirteen months of age, the child begins to communicate intentionally with the use of referential words and the construction of linguistic propositions. This is the locutionary (verbal) stage of communication. Thus, according to this framework, communication and language development are a three-staged process progressing from perlocutionary to illocutionary to locutionary communication.[7]

Individuals with profound intellectual disabilities communicate at all three levels. There are certainly those whose communication abilities develop to the illocutionary and locutionary stages, to the point of being able to employ preverbal gestures and/or referential words with the intent to communicate a particular need or want. An example of an individual with profound intellectual disabilities communicating at the illocutionary stage is one who learns to hum and look alternately at her caregiver and a plate of food during mealtime as a signal for "more."[8] Intentionality cannot be measured directly in individuals who communicate at this level. It must be inferred from observable behaviors displayed during interactions.[9] Thus, Siegel and Wetherby measure intentional communication operationally, based on a set of behavioral criteria, such as alternating gaze between the goal and the listener, awaiting a response from the listener, and changing the signal quality until the goal has been met.[10] In the previous example, intentionality must be inferred through observation of the individual's behavior, including her humming in conjunction with her gaze alternating between the food and her caregiver. An obvious illustration of an individual communicating at the locutionary stage is one who turns his head and says "no" when his caregiver offers to give him oral medication. Individuals communicating at both the illocutionary and locutionary stages employ sounds, sentences, words, gestures, and the like with the intent to communicate a desire or need to others. In Kaufman's terms, they demonstrate the capacity to employ symbolic material sufficiently to engage in intentional agency. Their behavior reflects the capacity for symbolization of self and other necessary to envision a goal and intend to accomplish it. They would be considered human given Kaufman's understanding of the term, though one must assume their humanity has yet to "mature" since their capacity for agency is limited as a result of their limited symbolic skills.[11] Individuals communicating at these levels would also be considered human given Lindbeck's understanding of the concept, since they demonstrate the ability to express themselves using symbols with the intent to give meaning to experience.

The population of individuals with profound intellectual disabilities with whom I am concerned in this book includes those whose communicative abilities remain at the perlocutionary stage, whose behavior serves a communicative function as it affects and evokes a response from the caregiver, without the production of signals with the intent to communicate. An example of an individual with a profound intellectual disability communicating at this stage is an individual who squeals, turns his gaze in the direction of the window, and increases motor activity at the sound of the children playing in the schoolyard across the street (as when an infant attends to the sound of a musical mobile hanging above her crib). There is no sign of intentional communication here, as this individual's gaze remains in the direction of the children's voices, he does not await a response from his caregiver, and there is no change in the quality of his behavior until he gets a response from his caregiver. Rather, it is up to his caregiver to respond to this behavior, as if the individual with the disability were communicating that he wants to watch the children play, and then to position that individual's wheelchair closer to the window. Individuals communicating at this level pose a challenge to Kaufman and Lindbeck's conceptions of what it means to be human, because their behavior does not reveal an ability to employ symbols of self and other necessary to envision a goal and act with the intent to accomplish it (in Kaufman's terms); neither does their behavior reveal an ability to express themselves symbolically with the intent to give meaning to their experience (using Lindbeck's terms). They do, however, express the ability to participate in mutually responsive relationships—to respond to the world around them and to evoke a response from others. As I will demonstrate, it is this participation in responsive relations that expresses their status as fully human.

THE RELATIONALITY OF CHAN: A PHENOMENOLOGY

Now that we have a framework for understanding the level of ability to respond or communicate on the part of the individuals with whom I am concerned in this book, let me now turn to a phenomenological description of the relationality of an individual with profound intellectual disabilities whom I will name Chan. I will begin with a description of Chan's disability, including the level of his cognitive and functional disabilities. I will follow with a description of the ways in which Chan responds to the world around him. Chan is a twenty-year-old man born with cerebral palsy. He is profoundly intellectually disabled, which involves intellectual functioning at an IQ level of below 20 or 25,[12] as well as severe impairments in adaptive behavior.[13] In terms of his level of communication, Chan's behavior does not indicate the ability to comprehend words or sentences; neither is he able to produce them. He does not demonstrate an ability to use gestures or sounds with the intent to communicate his needs or wants. Developmentally, Chan remains at the level of an infant; he did not achieve major developmental milestones such as rolling from prone to supine or vice versa, maintaining an upright head position when sitting or being held, sitting unsupported, crawling, or walking. He is totally dependent on his caregiver for the provision of his basic needs. He remains either in his bed at night or sitting up in his wheelchair during the daytime, with numerous supports to maintain a midline position of his head and trunk. As a result of his cerebral palsy, Chan has spastic quadriplegia, which means that he has poor motor control of his extremities and his movements are uncoordinated. Chan lives in a group home owned by the state in which he lives. He has a caregiver, Philip, who is employed by the state. Philip lives with Chan in the group home, along with three other men with profound intellectual disabilities and their caregivers. Philip provides for Chan's daily needs, such as feeding, bathing, dressing, and transferring him to and from his bed and wheelchair. Philip also provides transportation for Chan to and from the day treatment center where Chan socializes with other people with intellectual disabilities and receives therapy services.

Despite the limitations in Chan's cognitive and functional abilities, there are significant abilities that Chan does have. Primary among them is Chan's ability to express himself in a variety of ways and to interact with the world around him. The caregivers in Chan's group home have noticed that when Philip enters Chan's room in the mornings to bathe, dress, and transfer him to the wheelchair, Chan exhibits more "awake behavior." The motor activity of his arms and legs increases, his eyes remain open, he smiles, and he begins to vocalize at the sound of Philip's voice. However, when another caregiver enters his room and begins to bathe and dress him, if Philip is ill or has a day off, for example, Chan demonstrates less "awake behavior." He is less easily aroused. His eyes open only intermittently when the other caregivers try to arouse him, and he grinds his teeth while he is awake, as he often does while he is asleep. While new caregivers who are not familiar with Chan and his relationship to Philip initially interpret this sleep behavior as "problem" behavior, Philip and the more experienced caregivers view this change in behavioral state as a form of communication.[14] They have learned over the years of observing Chan's behavior to interpret this awake/asleep pattern in relation to Philip's presence as an expression of Chan's familiarity with Philip, and they make every effort to ensure that Philip is the one who bathes and dresses Chan every day. Although Chan demonstrates no awareness that this behavior affects others (for example, he continues the sleep behavior even after the other caregivers have left the room; the sleep behavior does not intensify if Philip remains absent), it appears that Chan responds very differently to his normal caregiver, Philip, from how he does to the other caregivers. As Philip bathes and dresses him, Chan's gaze intermittently turns in the direction of Philip. His awake behavior persists as Philip talks to him and transfers him to his wheelchair.

In the evenings, a similar situation occurs. Philip and the other caregivers have noticed that once Philip transfers Chan from his wheelchair to his bed and changes him into his bedclothes, Chan often remains awake unless Philip is in the room. If Philip is present as Chan is preparing to sleep, Chan's heart rate decreases and his muscle spasms diminish so that the position of his arms and legs release from a flexed position to a more extended, relaxed one. He falls asleep more often and more quickly when Philip is present. Though Chan does not appear to be aware of the ways in which his behavior affects Philip or the other caregivers (for example, his muscle tone remains hyper regardless of whether someone is present in the room), it appears that Chan's behavioral states are associated with his relationship to Philip. He wakes in the morning and falls asleep at night more readily with Philip's presence.

Chan responds in similar ways during his work with his physical therapist at the day treatment center. Philip brings Chan to meet his physical therapist, Sara, in the physical therapy gym each weekday morning. As Sara enters the room, Chan's eye movements increase, his head position rotates left and right, and he is more alert. Philip and Sara interpret this to mean that Chan is aware of Sara's presence. Sara greets Chan and explains that she is taking him to the mat where they can do exercises, as they do with each visit.[15] When Sara transfers Chan from the wheelchair to the mat, she notices the spasticity in his limbs has increased. This is often the case after Sara transfers Chan, which she interprets as expressive of his experience of the transfer as unstable and insecure. To diminish the spasticity and to help Chan feel more secure, Sara asks Philip to kneel behind Chan to help him maintain a seated, upright, midline position of his trunk and head. Sara places a very large yellow ball in Chan's lap and positions his arms on top of the ball. Seated on a stool in front of Chan, Sara slowly and gently rocks Chan forward and backward. As she does this, she notices that Chan's arms offer less resistance to their extended position on the ball, and that the spasticity of his legs release as Chan settles into the seated position with his hips and knees flexed and his feet flat on the floor.

Once Chan's spasticity has diminished, Sara proceeds with Chan's therapeutic program of engaging in activity that will help to facilitate muscle tone sufficient to support his head and trunk in a midline, upright, seated position. With Chan seated on the mat, Sara supports his shoulders as she leans him to the left, halfway between an upright and a side-lying position. In response, Sara notes that Chan's head, though in a flexed position due to his poor head control, turns slightly in the direction of an upright position. She also notices his right leg minimally elevating and his trunk musculature activating to pull his shoulders toward the upright position. Sara interprets Chan's efforts to "right" the position of his body to midline in response to her positioning him outside of midline as expressive of Chan's ability to be aware of the position of his body in space and to act in a way that promotes a midline, upright position. Sara responds to Chan's efforts to "right" the position of his body by returning him to an upright, midline position and offering him words of encouragement and praise. Though Chan does not respond appropriately to this verbal communication (by giving a smile in response to Sara's praise, for instance), Sara knows that it is important to respond to Chan's efforts to right himself by completing the task for him and offering him words of praise, as it is interactions such as these that will help Chan's preintentional communicative efforts develop into intentional ones.[16] Eventually, Sara hopes, Chan will develop the awareness that he has some control over his body position, as well as the awareness of the effect that his behavior has on others.

In an effort to promote better head control, Sara then positions Chan on the mat in a prone-on-elbows position with his upper body resting on a firm wedge-shaped pillow. Initially, Chan's head remains in a flexed position, with his eyes focused on the floor of the mat. Knowing that Chan is especially responsive to Philip's presence, Sara positions Philip in front of Chan. She asks Philip to speak to Chan as he usually does, in an effort to encourage Chan to elevate his head to a position from which he can view Philip's face. Sara notices the increased activity in the muscles along the back of Chan's neck as his head slightly elevates and the gaze of his eyes moves upward in the direction of Philip's face. After several seconds in which Chan attempts to elevate the position of his head in an upright position, Sara intervenes and assists Chan in the completion of this task. Although Chan does not have the control of his ocular muscles sufficient to maintain his gaze on any object for an extended period of time, he intermittently positions his eyes at Philip until Sara slowly lets go of Chan's head and allows it to return to a flexed position, with his gaze directed at the floor of the mat.

Sara and Chan repeat this activity several times, alternating between facilitating an upright head position from which Chan attends to Philip's face, a bright orange ball, or any other favorite object and returning to a flexed head position with his gaze directed at the floor of the mat. As is often the case, after thirty minutes or so of a variety of therapy activities, Chan's behavioral state begins to change. He becomes difficult to arouse, with his eyes remaining closed. He often becomes incontinent at this point, which results in an interruption in the therapy session while Philip cleans Chan and changes his clothes. Despite his having been cleaned and changed, Chan's sleep behavior persists. Sara interprets this behavior as expressive of Chan's feeling tired and uninterested in continuing the therapy session. Sara ends the session at this time and tells Chan she will see him at their next scheduled appointment.

Toward the end of the day, Philip transports Chan to the common room in the day treatment center where many other individuals with intellectual disabilities and their caregivers congregate for a time to socialize. Philip positions Chan's wheelchair against a wall near a television, where Philip proceeds to watch the local news broadcast. Meanwhile, a noisy game of volley with a balloon has begun across the room, involving both caregivers and individuals with intellectual disabilities. As the game proceeds, Chan begins to vocalize, his head flexes forward and backward, and the motor activity of his arms and legs increases. Philip notices the change in Chan's behavior and interprets it to mean that Chan is interested in what is going on across the room. Philip proceeds to move Chan's wheelchair over to the group playing the game so that Chan can participate with Philip's help. Even though he is unable to participate in the volleying of the balloon, Chan is able to participate through his presence as he responds to the game being played with changes in his behavior, which Philip and the others interpret as Chan's interest in the activity.

There is no evidence in this case study that Chan employs symbols as he relates to Philip, Sara, or the other individuals at the day treatment center. There is no evidence that he uses preverbal gestures with the intent to communicate a need or want (illocutionary stage of communication). Chan exhibits none of the behavioral criteria that Siegel and Wetherby employ to identify intentional communication, such as an alternating gaze between the goal and the listener, awaiting a response from the listener, or changing the signal quality until the goal has been met. And, clearly, Chan does not communicate intentionally with the use of referential words or the construction of linguistic propositions (locutionary stage of communication). Rather, it is evident that Chan is communicating at a preintentional level (perlocutionary stage of communication). Chan does respond to the world around him through changes in his behavior, and the world around him in turn responds to him. However, these changes in Chan's behavior appear to serve a communicative function, not because they are an intentional attempt by Chan to communicate but because they are interpreted by those language users around him as expressive of wants and needs of which Chan appears to be unaware. For example, Chan's sleep behavior does not intensify if Philip leaves his room, as an attempt to accomplish the goal of communicating his desire for Philip to remain present. Chan does respond to Philip by waking in the morning and falling asleep at night with his presence, but there is no indication that this behavior is used by Chan to communicate intentionally a desire for Philip's presence. As another example, Chan's efforts to right his head and trunk as he sits on the physical therapy mat do not intensify nor does he alternate his gaze between Sara's face and the direction of a midline position of his trunk until Sara returns him to an upright, midline sitting position. Chan does respond to Sara's changing the position of his body by attempting to return to midline, but there is no indication that he uses this behavior with the intent to communicate to Sara his desire for her to return him to midline.

One could respond at this point that while there is no evidence that Chan communicates intentionally, it is possible that his actions still express intentionality. Although his actions may not be expressive of his intent to communicate to a particular person, one could argue, they may still be expressive of his intent to accomplish a particular goal, such as sitting in an upright position, or having Philip in the room. The change in his behavior in response to the game being played across the room may not be expressive of his intention to communicate to someone else a desire to participate in the game, but one could argue that the behavior is still expressive of Chan's intention to join the game. My response to this argument is that one could conceive of this as intentional behavior, if by that we mean behavior that expresses simply the awareness of that which is outside the self or the awareness of the position of the body in space. This would be behavior that is shared by a newborn infant as she stirs at the sound of a parent's voice, or as she attempts to elevate her head to see the world around her. The question here, however, is not whether individuals with profound intellectual disabilities are aware of the world around them or of the position of their bodies within it. Chan's behavior in response to Philip's or Sara's presence, for example, appears to indicate an awareness of a change in his surroundings, and Chan's efforts to right the position of his body in response to Sara's positioning him out of midline appear to indicate an awareness of a change in the position of his body in space. The question, rather, is whether these individuals are aware that they are aware. Does their behavior indicate that they are aware that the world exists outside themselves or that their bodies are in a particular position in space? This is the level of intellectual ability Kaufman considers necessary for understanding what it means to be human: the ability for self-reflection, to symbolize the self as distinct from the other, and thus the ability to symbolize a goal as outside the self and to act with the intent to accomplish it. The behavior of individuals like Chan, though expressive of an awareness of the world around them, does not indicate that they have the self-awareness necessary to act with intentionality as Kaufman understands the term. We have discussed the evidence that Chan does not possess the self-awareness necessary to communicate intentionally (using Kaufman's sense of the term); he does not alternate his gaze between Sara and the location of an upright, midline position in an effort to communicate to her his desire to sit upright, for example, even though his behavior indicates that he was attempting to sit upright. But this lack of self-awareness is evident in all of Chan's behavior, and not only in those behaviors with the potential to serve a social, communicative function. There is no evidence of planning his behaviors in an attempt to accomplish a particular goal, persisting at a particular behavior until a goal is met or changing his behavior when a particular plan of action is not successful. Chan's behaviors in response to the world around him remain diffuse, with little evidence of an awareness of the ways in which his behaviors may affect the world outside of himself.

My point, however, is not to emphasize an ability that Chan lacks, namely, the ability to conceive of self and other. My point, rather, is to reveal the ways in which responsive relations are possible for individuals without the intellectual capacity for conceptualization, and thereby to suggest an alternative understanding of what it means to be human based on these responsive relations. Even though Chan's behavior indicates that he does not employ symbols or gestures with the intent to communicate, and even though his behavior indicates that he does not possess the self-awareness necessary to act with the intent to accomplish a particular goal, Chan's behavior does indicate that he is able to respond to the world around him, and those around him respond in turn to the changes in Chan's behavior. Chan's attempt to right himself in midline in response to Sara's positioning him out of midline does not intensify when he is unsuccessful nor does he try an alternative method (such as reaching for Sara's arms) as an indication of his awareness that he is sitting out of midline or of his goal of returning to midline. Neither does he alternate his gaze between Sara and the location of a midline sitting position as if to communicate to her his desire to sit upright. He does respond to Sara's positioning him out of midline, however, with visible efforts to realign his body in the upright position, and Sara responds in turn by helping Chan return to midline and praising him for his efforts. Similarly, Chan does not try an alternative behavior, such as screaming or biting, when his sleep behavior does not accomplish the goal of replacing a new caregiver with Philip's presence, and his sleep behavior does not intensify in an effort to accomplish this goal. However, he does respond differently to Philip's presence in the mornings (with awake behavior) than he does to other caregivers (with sleep behavior), and his caregivers respond in kind by doing their best to ensure Philip's presence in the morning and at bedtime. As a final example, Chan's motor activity and vocalizations do not intensify until he joins the game of balloon volley as an expression of his goal of participating in the game; neither does he alternate his gaze between Philip and the game in an effort to communicate to Philip his desire to move his wheelchair closer to the game. However, Chan does respond to the sounds and sights of the game with changes in his behavior, such as vocalizing and increasing the motor activity of his body. Philip then responds to this change in behavior by interpreting it as an expression of Chan's desire to participate, and he proceeds to move Chan's wheelchair closer to the activity.

Chan's ability to participate in responsive relations such as these, and yet without the ability to conceive of himself as a self that is distinct from the world around him, suggests that an anthropology different from that of Lindbeck and Kaufman is needed. If we are to conceive of individuals with Chan's level of intellectual ability as fully human, we need a way of thinking about what it means to be human other than Lindbeck's emphasis on the ability to express oneself symbolically using public gestures or words with the intent to give meaning or experience or Kaufman's emphasis on the capacity to employ concepts of self and other required for intentional agency. We need an anthropology that is broad enough to consider individuals without the intellectual capacity to perform these symbolizing functions as fully human, and not deficiently so.

In this book, I suggest that we turn to the responsive relations of individuals with profound intellectual disabilities as a resource for reconceiving what it means to be human. Employing Kaufman's methodology of constructing theological concepts that are relevant given a broad range of human situations, I suggest that the situation of the profoundly intellectually disabled among us calls us to reconsider our traditional conceptions of what it means to be human and that only by taking this population into account will our anthropology be a just one. Through a phenomenological description of the relational life of one individual with a profound intellectual disability, I have attempted to display the ways in which mutually responsive relationships are possible for these individuals, even when symbolization and conceptualization are not. Given this relationality, I suggest that we no longer conceive of what it means to be human in terms of the capacity for symbolization or conceptualization. Rather, I suggest that we conceive of human being as a relational concept, as involving the capacity for responsiveness, but always a responsiveness in relation to an other and never the capacity for responsiveness in and of itself.

In an effort to develop this alternative anthropology, I turn to dialogical philosophy as a resource. Here human being is conceived not as a static concept, as defined by the possession of a particular capacity, such as the intellectual ability to reflect on the world—to categorize and qualify it. Rather, human being is a dynamic concept, involving responsiveness to the Thou we encounter. Human being is not defined by the possession of the intellectual capacity to employ concepts of self and other necessary to act with intention or to give meaning to experience. Human being is understood in terms of the participation in relationships of mutual responsiveness. In the following chapter, I will discuss the dialogical philosophy of Martin Buber and its relevance for my efforts to think of human being in terms mindful of the full humanity of individuals with profound intellectual disabilities. Given the phenomenological description of the responsive relations of Chan in this chapter, I will argue that Buber's understanding of human being in terms of meeting the other in relationship of mutuality, totalization, and immediacy, rather than in terms of some capacity, intellectual or otherwise, is broad enough to acknowledge the full humanity of individuals with profound intellectual disabilities.

4. Martin Buber's Anthropology

FOR MARTIN BUBER, there is no "nature of human being" in the sense of some isolatable capacity or metaphysical substance, such as the soul, located within an individual human being. Any attempt to understand human being in this way, in fact, runs contrary to the meaning of the concept. Rather, for Buber, human being can be understood only in terms of participation in relations, which he often described using the linguistic metaphor of "dialogue." He was not the first to conceive of human being in this way. The nineteenth-century philosopher Ludwig Feuerbach also understood human being not in terms of some isolatable capacity or metaphysical substance located within the individual but as participation in the relationship of human being to human being, in the I and Thou.[1] During Buber's years as a student at the University of Vienna, one of his teachers, F. Jodl, was an editor of Feuerbach's works. It has been suggested that Feuerbach influenced Buber's work as a result of his studies with Jodl.[2] A number of Buber's contemporaries were also thinking in dialogical terms, including H. Cohen, F. Ebner, and G. Marcel, though the evidence of dialogical thought in Buber's works appears as early as 1905, much earlier than works by these three authors.[3] Despite this shared interest in dialogical thought, the distinctness of Buber's work lies in his determination to remain focused on the concreteness of the world of actual human relations. He is intent upon remaining within "the stream" of life and giving a philosophical account of what is experienced from within that life.[4] As a result, Buber expressed his skepticism about philosophical systems and even the philosophical attitude itself. His work has been criticized for lacking a systematic philosophical grounding; Buber himself admits the truth of this criticism.[5] But Buber remains unapologetic. He criticized the abstract modes of philosophizing for removing us from the concrete world, from the stream of life. "Here you do not attain to knowledge by remaining on the shore . . . you must make the venture and cast yourself in . . . in this way, and in no other, do you reach anthropological insight."[6] Buber eschewed abstract concepts and ideas and turned to the world of concrete relations as the focal point of his philosophy and the primary location for his insight into the meaning of human being.

As a result of Buber's observations of concrete human relations, he identified two modes of discourse, or "words," that reflect the two basic attitudes that human beings take or movements they make in relation to whomever or whatever she or he meets. The first movement, *Ruckbiegung* or "bending back to oneself," develops into the attitude where the Other exists as a value-neutral object for the projects of the self. The word reflecting this basic attitude is what Buber called I-It. The second movement, *Hinwendung* or "turning toward the Other," develops into the attitude in which the Other is valued for itself and is allowed to put its own claim on the self. The word reflecting this basic attitude is I-Thou.[7]

For Buber, our wholeness as human beings cannot be found through participation in I-It relations. He writes, "The primary word I-It can never be spoken with the whole being."[8] This is because the otherness that is manifest in these relations is not that of the Other as Other but as the Other-for-me, and if the Other as Other cannot be wholly manifest here, neither can the wholeness of the self. The Other that is manifest here is as an object for the use of the self, as based on biological, sensorial, perspectival, or intellectual functions of the self.[9] Michael Theunissen speaks of the sphere of I-It relations as the "sphere of subjectivity" in which all entities are oriented toward the I as the acting subject and as the center point of the world, which she or he intentionally dominates. This is akin to the master-slave relationship in which the domination is not external domination but the domination of the constituting capacity of the subject that orders all entities in accordance with the intentional acts of the I.[10] As a result of this world-dominating subjectivity, the Other as Other is lost, being manifest as a function of the intentions of the I and not as it truly is in and of itself. The important point here is not only that otherness cannot be wholly manifest here, but also that as a consequence of its world-dominating functions the wholeness of the self cannot be manifest either. Because there is no specifiable I without the Other in virtue of which the I is specifiable, the wholeness of the self cannot be manifest in I-It relations.[11] It should be noted that it is not the case, for Buber, that I-It relations serve no function for human beings. In fact, he argues that human beings cannot live without them; these relations give human beings the ability to order their world and their sense of security within it.[12] It is only that these relations are insufficient to sustain human existence.

Human existence is to be found for Buber through participation in I-Thou relations where the fullness of both the I and the Thou meet. Our humanity exists where the undivided I and the undivided Thou meet, in the realm of what Buber refers to as "the between."[13] Buber's I-Thou relation involves immediacy, totalization, the coming together of will and grace, and mutuality. In contrast to I-It relations[14] in which there is mediation of the It through the world-constituting intentional acts of the subject, I-Thou relations involve an immediacy of relation between I and Thou. There is no reflecting, categorizing or ordering of the Thou on the part of the I here, and there are no concepts or ideas that mediate the relation between them. In Buber's words, "The relation to the Thou is direct. No system of ideas, no foreknowledge and no fancy . . . no aim, no lust, and no anticipation intervene between I and Thou. . . . Every means is an obstacle. Only when every means has collapsed does the meeting come about."[15]

Closely related to this immediacy, for Buber, is the idea of presence. When we reflect on the Other we encounter, we mediate our relation to it by referring to similar things in our past or fitting it into our future projects. In the process, we objectify the Other as it becomes a mirror of the structures of our knowing-desiring self. We reduce the presence of the Other to the past as its uniqueness is considered only in terms of what it has in common with others we have encountered. The important distinction here is between object and presence. When we reflect on the Other, we see ourselves as "here" and the Other as "there," as the object of our reflection.[16] What is lost with reflection, however, is the mutual presence of the subject and object to each other. For Buber, preceding their separation through reflection, the subject and object are present to each other without mediation of concepts, categories, and ideas.[17] Again, it is not the case, for Buber, that objectification of the Other has no role to play in the I-Thou relation. Through reflection, we categorize and organize the other in a way that enlarges the I of the Other and provokes a more profound meeting. The concern here, for Buber, is that through objectification of the Other we lose the capacity to be aware of the sheer presence of the Other.[18] At this point, mutual relations, and thereby our existence as human beings, disappear.

The work of the social phenomenologist Alfred Schutz offers help here in understanding the immediacy of Buber's I-Thou relation. Schutz designates social relations with the expression "we-relations," which involve living in and being absorbed in common experiences with an Other.[19] They are characterized by temporal and spatial immediacy and are built up in our experience upon the face-to-face encounter with the Other. "I immediately perceive another man only when he shares a sector of the life-world's space and of world time in common with me . . . he and I grow old together."[20] Only with body-to-body, face-to-face encounter, according to Schutz, is it possible for the immediacy of the we-relation to occur.

Like Buber's I-Thou relation, the we-relation may be interrupted with reflective activity. I place myself outside of the we-relation when I turn from living within our common experience and attempt to explicate the movements, expressions, and communications of the Other as indications of their subjective experiences. "When I turn reflectively to our experiences, then I have, so to speak, placed myself outside of the we-relation."[21] At this point, the Other whom I initially experienced immediately in the we-relation is now distanced from me as that Other becomes the object of my reflective activity. Similarly with Buber's dialogical philosophy, the immediacy of the I-Thou relation is lost as I reflect on the Other and mediate my relation to it by comparing it to similar objects in my past or fitting it into my future projects. For both Schutz and Buber, the immediate experience of an Other is hindered by my perspectival, reflective activity.

What is helpful about Schutz's account of the structures of the social world, and what Buber seems to take for granted, is that Schutz acknowledges outright the importance of spatial and temporal immediacy in social relations. It is only within body-to-body, face-to-face encounter that we perceive the Other with immediacy. Schutz offers a highly organic account of what lies at the basis of the social world, and he indicates what I think Buber infers when he speaks of the subject and object as present to one another without mediation of concepts, categories, or ideas. Preceding their separation through reflection, the I and Thou encounter one another in temporal and spatial immediacy, body-to-body and face-to-face, with awareness of the sheer presence of the Other.

Schutz grants that any encounter with the Other in the we-relation must necessarily be manifested bodily. I make myself known to and experienced by the Other by means of my bodily expression. Conversely, the Other makes herself known to and experienced by me solely via her bodily expressions. Thus, in a sense, for Schutz the we-relation, while immediate, is also a mediated one.[22] This leads to Schutz's curious claim that the mediacy here is so close, is indeed "simultaneous," that "we will continue to speak, even though it is not completely accurate, of an immediate experience of the fellow-man."[23] Thus, Schutz concedes to a bodily mediation of the we-relation, but it is mediation that is freed from reflective activity, and in this sense it is immediate. "This immediacy is preserved only as long as I live in the we-relation. . . . When I turn reflectively to our experiences, then I have, so to speak, placed myself outside of the we-relation."[24]

Along with the characteristic of immediacy, the I-Thou relation involves an indistinguishable fusing of all characteristics of the Thou, for Buber—what Robert E. Wood refers to as "totalization."[25] Granted, the encounter involves a number of identifiable characteristics of the Thou, but with the I-Thou relation the attention of the I is on the whole of the Other and not any isolatable characteristic. This encounter involves a unique kind of knowing that is different from the reflective, categorizing attention to detail of the I-It relation. It is a knowing of uniqueness that is a requisite for saying Thou, which Buber refers to as "seeing the whole" or "synthesizing apperception."[26] With the I-Thou relation, the I leaves behind the reflective, categorizing activity of the I-It relation and meets the Thou as whole to whole. In Buber's words, "What, then, do we know of the Thou? Just everything. For we know nothing isolated about it anymore."[27]

For Buber, in order for this totalization, this knowing of the whole-ness of the Thou to occur, both will and grace is required. Meeting the Thou requires both my activity and my passivity, my choosing and being chosen.[28] It requires my activity as I go my own way and meet the Thou, in the sense that I must go out and await its presence.[29] But it requires more than my activity alone. Ultimately, meeting the Thou requires activity on the part of the Thou as the Thou is going his own way and meets me. This is grace in the sense that the meeting cannot take place as a result of my own act alone; it requires that the Thou give itself to me.[30] Thus, meeting the Thou requires both will and grace, for Buber. It can just as well never happen "without me" as it can "never happen through me."[31] Meeting, for Buber, can never occur as a result of my own act alone; it requires cooperation on the part of the Thou who presents himself to me.[32]

As a result of this interaction of will and grace, a mutuality occurs in the I-Thou relation in which the I affects the Thou and the Thou affects the I. "My Thou affects me, as I affect it."[33] Buber speaks of the effect of the I on the Thou in terms of a response of love to the Thou, not as a matter of feeling but as a participation in the meeting. Feelings may accompany love, but they do not constitute it. If love were a feeling, it would cling to the I in such a way that the Thou would be merely an "object" of the feeling of the I. Rather, Buber conceives of love as that which is between I and Thou, as that which takes place in the meeting. In the eyes of the one who takes his stand in love, the Other is set free from the oppressive effects of the scrutinizing, categorizing I and confronts the I as Thou. In this I-Thou relation, the I ceases its perspectival attention to the particular qualities of the Other and responds instead to the wholeness of the Other. Here the Other emerges not as object of the perspectival functions of the I but as the Thou of relation. And as a result of this loving response of meeting between the I and the Thou, real effectiveness occurs, which Buber describes as helping, healing, educating, raising up, and saving.[34] Without full responsiveness, however, one affects the other only partially and superficially.[35]

It is important to note two things here. First, in his discussion of the effect of the I on the Thou, Buber refers not only to human-to-human relations but also to human relations with animals and with nature.

He does not specify the effect of our response on that which is not human; this remains "sunk in mystery."[36] But Buber does make clear that when one responds lovingly to the wholeness of these beings in their totality, God's glory will be manifest in them.[37] In Buber's words, "man is commissioned and summoned as a cosmic mediator to awaken a holy reality in things through holy contact with them."[38] And second, although his attention is turned primarily to the effect of the I on the Thou, Buber's point here is that I-Thou relations involve a mutuality of effects. "Relation is mutual. My Thou affects me, as I affect it."[39] Thus, he writes, "we are moulded by our pupils," "the 'bad' man, lightly touched by the holy primary word, becomes one who reveals," and "how we are educated by our children and by animals!"[40] For Buber, not only do we bring knowledge, healing, and help to the Thou we encounter, but the Thou affects us in similar ways as well.

One of the primary metaphors Buber uses to discuss the mutuality of I-Thou relations is "dialogue."[41] Buber describes the dialogical character of the I-Thou relation as involving the experience of being addressed and answering a word and response—"a word demanding an answer has happened to me."[42] This experience of being addressed and of responding involves responsibility, for Buber, in two senses. The first is that of responding to a call; the second is that of being supposed to respond. This second sense of responsibility is not the juristic sense of one's being supposed to account for one's deeds. Rather, it is responsibility in the sense of having to live up to what is essential to being human—responding to the one who addresses me.[43] He writes, "The idea of responsibility is to be brought back from the province of specialized ethics, of an 'ought' that swings free in the air, into that of lived life. Genuine responsibility exists only where there is real responding."[44] Thus, responsibility for Buber does not have a narrow, impersonal, moralistic meaning. Rather, Buber conceives of responsibility as rooted in our very nature as human beings.[45] He writes, "Responsibility presupposes one who addresses me primarily, that is, from a realm independent of myself, and to whom I am answerable."[46] "Answerable" here refers to responsibility not as a moral obligation to respond but in Buber's second sense as indicating that we are bound to act in a certain way in response to one who addresses us because it is of the essence of human life that we do so.[47]

Buber's claim that we find our humanity in our responsiveness to the Thou we encounter signals his position that the mutuality of effects of the I-Thou relation includes not only bringing knowledge, help, and healing to the partners of the dialogue. The mutuality of effects also includes Buber's idea of the reciprocal constitution of the I and the Thou; the birth of the partners comes out of the event of meeting.[48] In Buber's words, "human being becomes an I on account of the Thou."[49] This can have only a conceptual meaning, for Buber, and not a factual one. Otherwise, Buber's understanding of the reciprocal constitution of the I and the Thou would be incomprehensible. If we take Buber literally, in order to constitute the Thou, the I would have to already exist. But Buber's theory of reciprocal constitution includes the claim that the I cannot exist without the Thou, which it first has to constitute. To make sense of his theory, we must realize that it has nothing to do with the existence of things in isolation from each other. It has to do rather with our existence as persons, which occurs simultaneously in the event of meeting, in mutually responsive relations in which I effects Thou and Thou effects I.[50]

This distinction between our existence in isolation from each other and our existence as persons goes back to Buber's original distinction between I-It and I-Thou relations. With each of the two basic attitudes human beings take toward the world, Buber claims, the I is different. He writes, "the I of man is also twofold. For the I of the primary word I-Thou is a different I from that of the primary word I-It."[51] Buber refers to the I of the I-It relation as *Eigenwesen* or the "individual."[52] The Individual is one who approaches the Other from the perspective of his or her own wants, needs, desires. "He constantly interposes his subjective designs between himself and reality and thus becomes incapable of listening and responding to whatever might meet him out of the situation."[53] The I of the I-Thou relation, by contrast—which Buber refers to as "person"[54] or "human being"[55]—engages the Other in open sharing in that which transcends itself. She is defined not by her own perspectival functions but in terms of the Other to which she responds.[56] Thus, it is to our existence as persons that Buber refers with his theory of the reciprocal constitution of the I and the Thou. It is not the case that the partners exist on a factual level as a result of the I-Thou relation. Rather, for Buber, their existence as persons, as responsive, nonobjectifying partners in dialogue, is constituted out of the relation to one another.

As was the case with the effect of bringing knowledge, healing, and help to the partners in I-Thou relations, the effect of being constituted by the relation applies mutually to both partners of the I-Thou relation. Buber's claim that "human being becomes an I on account of the Thou"[57] applies both to the Thou, insofar as he or she is a human being, as well as to the I. Thus, both the I and the Thou come to be on account of the Other. Buber leaves open two possibilities here. "I" come to be either in being addressed by my Thou, or in addressing my Thou. Similarly, the Thou becomes an I in that either she or he is addressed by me or addresses me.[58] In either case, whether one locates the Thou in addressing or being addressed, the salient point here is that for Buber both partners in the dialogue come to be as persons in the event of their meeting.

THE SIGNIFICANCE OF BUBER'S ANTHROPOLOGY FOR INDIVIDUALS WITH INTELLECTUAL DISABILITIES

Given Buber's understanding of human being as a relational concept involving the characteristics of immediacy, totalization, will and grace, and mutuality, let me now turn to a discussion of the relevance of Buber's anthropology vis-à-vis individuals with profound intellectual disabilities. Though Buber does not elaborate on the significance of his thought for individuals like Chan, he does indicate that his anthropology applies in a unique way to such individuals. In response to Walter Blumenfeld's suspicion regarding the application of Buber's concept of human being to individuals other than the "mature, normal person," such as those with mental illness, small children, and "idiots," Buber states that the I-Thou relation establishes itself naturally in such individuals:

> I believe I have made sufficiently clear that that which concerns me does not belong to an upper story of human nature. I have shown in detail how the I-Thou relation establishes itself naturally, as it were,

in the small child as in "primitive" man. As for the so-called idiots
[*sic*], I have many times perceived how the soul of such a man extends
its arms —and thrusts into emptiness. On the other hand, I have, not
at all seldom, learned to know persons of a high spiritual grade whose
basic nature was to withhold themselves from others even if they let
this one and that one come near to him. No, I mean no "spiritual
elite," and yes, I mean man as man. Hindrances everywhere place
themselves in the way, from without and from within; it is heart-will
and grace in one that help us mature and awake men to overcome
them and grant us meeting.[59]

Buber's comments here reveal that the I-Thou relation is not
limited to those with developed intellectual abilities. He indicates, in
fact, that the I-Thou relation appears "naturally" in the relations of
individuals who are less developed intellectually. And, though
he speaks explicitly only once in his published works about the
application of his anthropology to individuals with intellectual
disabilities, Buber refers often to the life of a very small child as
revealing most clearly the I-Thou relation.[60] These references indicate
that participation in I-Thou relations, as an indicator of what it means
to be human, is not only accessible to individuals with limited
intellectual abilities but is also especially accessible to them.

In the remainder of this chapter, I take up Buber's suggestion that
I-Thou relations are accessible to "so-called idiots," and his numerous
references to the accessibility of I-Thou relations to small children, as
indications of the relevance of Buber's anthropology for individuals
with profound intellectual disabilities. Though Buber does not elaborate on this connection himself, I find that the references above and
the overall tenor and trajectory of Buber's thought indicate that he
would not resist such a connection. It is my position that his understanding of human being as participation in relationships of immediacy, totality, will and grace, and mutual responsiveness is relevant to
individuals with profound intellectual disabilities, because it is broad
enough to include their humanity as individuals who participate in
such relations. In the coming pages, I will demonstrate the connection
between Buber's anthropology and its relevance for individuals with
profound intellectual disabilities by discussing the ways in which an
individual like Chan participates in I-Thou relations, thereby revealing

their humanity as Buber conceives of the term. Given the broadness of Buber's anthropology and its relevance to individuals with profound intellectual disabilities, I will claim that Christian theologians must reconstruct their concept of the human in ways similar to Buber's concept in order to consider individuals with profound intellectual disabilities as fully human and not deficiently so.

Returning now to the case study of Chan, upon examination of his relationality we find evidence of his participation in each of Buber's characteristics of I-Thou relations: immediacy, totality, will and grace, and mutuality. As indicated earlier, for Buber I-Thou relations involve a directness in which the partners of the meeting encounter one another as undivided with undivided. There is no categorizing, organizing, or reflecting of any kind that mediates the relation between them. With I-It relations, however, the I engages in mental acts such as perceiving and comparing in which his or her attention is given to particular characteristics of the Other. Such acts involve mediation of the relation between the partners by the subjective, perspectival functions of the I and result in objectification of particular characteristics of the Other and a blindness to the Other as it is in itself. In the case of Chan, his behavior gives no indication that he is able to employ conceptual material sufficiently to perform the categorizing, organizing, objectifying functions of the I of I-It relations. He does not demonstrate an ability to comprehend symbolic material, such as gestures or referential words on the part of his caregivers and friends by responding appropriately to them; for example, he does not raise his head when Sara asks him to or smile in response to Sara's praise. Chan also does not demonstrate the ability to employ gestures or vocalizations with the intent to communicate; he does not alternate his gaze between Philip and the game of volley as an expression of his intent to communicate to Philip his desire to join the fun, nor does his behavior indicate the self-awareness necessary to envision a goal and act with the intent to accomplish it. His effort to reorient his body in midline, for example, does not intensify, nor does he try an alternative method when his effort is unsuccessful, as an expression of his ability to conceive of himself as a self with a goal outside himself. Without the ability to employ symbolic material necessary for conceiving of himself as a self distinct from the world around him, it is difficult to conceive of Chan as able to perform the objectifying functions of the categorizing, organizing I of I-It relations.

Despite Chan's limited ability to reflect upon the world around him, however, it is not the case that he remains disengaged from the world. We have noted the changes in Chan's behavioral state as others approach him: His motor activity increases, and he becomes more alert. We have noticed similar changes in his behavior in response to the sights and sounds of his friends playing balloon volley across the room: He begins to vocalize, his head flexes forward and backward, and the motor activity of his arms and legs increases. Although he does not demonstrate the ability to employ symbols of self and other necessary to perform the objectifying functions of the I of I-It relations, Chan's behavior does express that he is aware of those around him and that he responds to them. Given his ability to engage his caregivers and friends, through this awareness and responsiveness, and yet without the reflective categorizing and organizing functions of the I of I-It relations, it becomes possible to conceive of Chan's relationships as involving the immediacy characteristic of Buber's I-Thou relations. Buber's distinction between object and presence becomes relevant here. Through reflection upon the Other we encounter we see ourselves as "here" and the Other as "there." We distance ourselves from the Other as it is becomes an object for our reflection. As Buber sees it, this removes us from that initial, original, immediate bond between subject and object, which he refers to as presence.[61] As a result of Chan's inability to be aware of himself as distinct from the world around him, it is difficult to conceive of Chan's ability to distance himself from the Other as an object for reflection. Rather, Chan's awareness of and responsiveness to those around him would be more like the "being present" that Buber speaks of as characteristic of I-Thou relations.[62] While Chan may not be able to employ the concepts necessary to engage Philip or Sara as objects for reflection, his behavior does indicate the ability to be aware of their presence and to be present to them without the mediation of concepts, categories, or ideas.

Chan's apparent unmediated attentiveness to Philip and Sara also serves as evidence of his ability to participate in the totalization that characterizes Buber's I-Thou relations. As Buber sees it, the kind of attentiveness of I-Thou relations is different from the attentiveness of I-It relations. "Meeting is a lived relation of whole to whole, and it requires an entirely different act of attentiveness to sort out objectifiable characteristics from the meeting."[63] With the reflective attentiveness to the particularities of the Other characteristic of I-It relations, the Other is not seen as it is in itself. It is not seen as a whole being, but rather as an object of the particular perspectival, reflective functions of the I. With I-Thou relations, however, the Thou is affirmed as it is in itself. The attentiveness of the I is given not to any particular characteristic of the Other but to the Thou as a whole. As a result, the I knows the Thou in its totality while knowing nothing of its particularities.[64]

For individuals with the ability to perform the reflective functions of I-It relations, the particular characteristics of the Other become sorted out from the original I-Thou meeting.[65] This is "the melancholy of our fate" as Buber sees it, that for those with the ability to perform the reflective functions of I-It relations it is inevitable that "every Thou in our world must become an It."[66] These characteristics are eventually able to return to their unity, through a return to the participation in I-Thou relations, but only with great difficulty.[67] For individuals like Chan, however, who are not able to perform the reflective functions necessary to isolate, categorize, and organize particular qualities of the Other, their attentiveness appears to remain on the Thou as a totality. Chan does not appear to share the destiny of individuals with reflective abilities to objectify the beings that surround them. His behavior gives no indication of the ability to employ concepts of self and other necessary to reflect on the world around him. His behavior does indicate, however, that Chan is able to be aware of his surroundings and of changes in his surroundings. Chan responds to the presence of Sara as she enters the room with increased eye movements, rotating the position of his head and an overall increased alertness. He also responds to the presence of Philip's face and a bright orange ball by attempting to elevate his head to a position from which he can view them as he lies prone on the mat. Chan's ability to attend to the presence of beings and objects in the world around him, without performing the perspectival, reflective functions of the objectifying I, is an indication of his ability to relate to the world around him with the totalizing, nonreflective attention characteristic of Buber's I-Thou relations.

In order for this unmediated meeting of whole to whole to occur, as Buber sees it, both will and grace are required. The I-Thou relation requires my will in the sense of some activity on my part, but it also requires grace in the sense of activity on the part of the Thou that is beyond my control. What this activity is and how it relates to an individual like Chan depends on how we interpret Buber's comments on the matter. Buber speaks at times of ways in which the I prepares itself for the meeting, actions that draw the I out of its own subjective preoccupation and prepare it for the I-Thou encounter. One form of such preparation is what Buber names "inclusion," by which he means experiencing a shared event from the side of the Other with whom the event is shared.[68] With the effort to live through a common event from the standpoint of the other, the I prepares herself to overcome mere elaboration of her own subjectivity and to receive the presence of the Other as it is in itself. Because such inclusion first requires the ability to conceive of the self as distinct from the other, it is difficult to see how an individual like Chan might be able to participate in willing of this kind. To cognitively "step outside" of one's own experience and "step into" the experience of another requires a highly developed cognitive awareness of one's own self as an experiencing self, as well as an awareness of his or her distinction from the other as an experiencing self. Because this level of self-awareness is not accessible to an individual like Chan, it would not be possible for him to "prepare" himself for I-Thou relations by performing such acts of "inclusion." Despite the role these acts play in preparing the I for entering into relation, however, Buber does not consider them necessary for participation in I-Thou relations. In fact, there are a variety of I-Thou relations in which acts of inclusiveness occur on the part of only one partner in the meeting, as in the case of a teacher who is able to experience the student's being educated, while the student cannot experience the educating of the educator.[69]

Buber also speaks of the activity of "willing" in the sense of going my own way, awaiting the presence of the Thou and receiving it as Thou when the meeting happens.[70] It is Buber's understanding of "activity" or "willing" in this sense that becomes accessible to

individuals with profound intellectual disabilities. The I-Thou
relation, for Buber, does not require that I actively seek the Thou, who
must choose on his or her own to engage in the meeting. Rather,
it requires that I respond to the Thou I encounter by speaking the
primary word I-Thou to it.[71] It requires that I respond to the presence
of the Thou I encounter not with the reflective, objectifying awareness
that is characteristic of the I of I-It relations but with an awareness
of the wholeness of the Thou that characterizes the I of I-Thou
relations. Given Chan's ability to be aware of others and to respond to
them, and yet without the reflective activities of the objectifying I of
I-It relations, it is possible to conceive of his ability to participate in this
form of "willing" required of Buber's I-Thou relations.

It appears, in fact, that because of Chan's disability he would be
more likely to participate in this form of willing than an individual
with a higher level of intellectual ability. Because of his disability, both
its intellectual and physical aspects, Chan is not able to actively seek an
object for encounter. Though he is able to respond to changes in his
environment—for example, increased sleep behavior when he has a
caregiver other than Philip to dress him in the morning—his behavior
gives no indication that he uses gestures or sounds with the intent to
accomplish a goal, such as trying an alternative behavior such as biting
or screaming when his sleep behavior does not achieve the goal
of Philip's presence. Given this inability to perform goal-directed
behavior, Chan is unable to actively seek the Thou, which Buber
considers a hindrance to allowing the Thou to choose the meeting
freely. Moreover, given Chan's inability to employ concepts of self and
other necessary for goal-directed behavior, he is unable to perform the
reflective, objectifying functions that Buber also considers a hindrance
to the unmediated meeting of whole to whole involved in I-Thou
relations. The fact that Chan is responsive to and aware of the world
around him, and yet without objectifying, organizing, and categorizing it, indicates that he would more readily engage the Other with the
unmediated, totalizing awareness of an I-Thou relation than would an
individual with the higher level of cognitive functioning necessary for
reflective awareness.

For Buber, in addition to willing on the part of the I, grace
is required on the part of the Thou in order for the I-Thou relation

to occur. The I-Thou relation requires not only my activity as I go my own way, await the presence of the Thou, and receive it as Thou when it approaches me. It requires activity on the part of the Thou as well.[72] This activity is "grace" in the sense of action on the part of the Thou that is beyond my control. "Grace," for Buber, does not exclusively mean action in the form of a conscious choosing to enter relationship.[73] It also means "being bodied over against me," as a presence whom I encounter as a single whole and not as an object for my scrutiny. Buber speaks of this form of "grace" as that which obtains when I encounter objects in nature, such as a tree or an animal.[74] Though an animal may not have the level of consciousness necessary to deliberately choose to enter into relationship, an animal does give to the relationship, as "grace," in that it presents itself to me and calls for my loving response. Thus, the I-Thou relation requires my willing in the sense that I must respond to the Thou I encounter as Thou, but it requires grace as well in the sense that my response is not possible without the Other's first offering itself to me.

Given the broadness of Buber's conception of the grace that is required for I-Thou relations, it becomes clear that individuals like Chan are able to participate in such relations not only as I, through performing the "willing" function, but also as Thou, by offering "grace" as a presence whom I encounter. Although Chan may not be able to offer grace in the form of consciously choosing to enter into relationship, he would be able to offer grace in the form of his bodied presence which I encounter and which calls for my response. And although I could choose to respond to Chan as It, as an object for my reflection, or as Thou, as the being I encounter, an I-Thou encounter with Chan, as Buber sees such an encounter, would not be possible without Chan's first offering himself as a presence calling for my response.

As a result of this interchange of will and grace between the partners of the meeting, there is a mutuality of effects in which the I affects the Thou and the Thou affects the I.[75] Buber speaks of this in terms of a mutuality of helping, healing and educating, as well as a reciprocity of constitution of the I and the Thou, all of which occurs as a result of responding to the Other with the totality and immediacy characteristic of the I-Thou relation. By responding to the Other whom I encounter as Thou, without the objectifying reflectivity of the I of I-It relations, the Other emerges as it is in itself. The Other emerges not as an object for the reflective activity of the I but as the Thou of relation. And similarly, as my Other responds to me as his Thou, he encounters me not as an object for reflection but as a being calling for a response of immediacy and totality.

Chan's ability to respond to those around him, and yet without the objectifying reflectivity of the I of I-It relations, appears in a variety of ways in his interactions with others. We witness this in the simpler of Chan's responses, such as his response to being transferred by Sara from his wheelchair to the physical therapy mat. On being transferred, Chan initially responds with an increase in spasticity in his arms and legs; his arms and legs stiffen into an extended position making the seated position difficult. However, once Philip is positioned behind Chan as a source of support for Chan's trunk, and once Sara begins to slowly rock Chan forward and backward, Chan responds with a relaxation of the spasticity as his arms rest on the ball and his legs relax into a seated position with hips and knees flexed and feet flat on the floor. Chan gives no indication that he is responding to Sara as an object for reflection. He does not appear to vocalize or use gestures with the intent to communicate to her a sense of insecurity about being transferred: His spasticity does not further intensify when Sara continues with the transfer, and he does not try an alternative method of communication when the transfer continues, such as screaming or biting. And yet his behavior does change in response to Sara's physical interaction with him, which Sara then interprets as an expression of Chan's anxiety with the transfer.

Chan's ability to respond to those around him can be witnessed as well through changes in his behavioral state in relation to changes in his surroundings. After several minutes of therapeutic activities with Sara, Chan often demonstrates an increase in sleep behaviors, such as closing his eyes and decreasing movement in his limbs. He also frequently becomes incontinent of his bowel and bladder at this point. This combination of behaviors results in a disruption of the therapy session in order for Philip to clean Chan and change his clothes. Chan's behavior does not indicate that he uses this behavior with the intent to communicate to Sara his desire to achieve a particular goal: He does not employ a different behavior when the current behavior does not result in a termination of the therapy session. And yet Chan does consistently respond to an extended therapy session with changes in his behavioral state.

Chan also responds to Philip's presence or absence as he awakens in the morning with changes in his behavioral state. His behavior demonstrates a pattern of arousing with Philip's presence and remaining difficult to arouse in Philip's absence. Again in this case, Chan's behavior does not demonstrate that he is able to engage his caregivers as objects for reflection. The ability to reflect on the world outside the self requires the ability to conceive of the self as distinct from the world. This ability could be demonstrated by the employment of behavior with the intent to accomplish a desired goal. Chan's behavior does not demonstrate that he possesses this ability. While Chan does respond to Philip's presence or absence with a change in his behavioral state, he does not demonstrate an awareness of the effect this behavior has on the world around him. His sleep behavior does not intensify when a caregiver other than Philip bathes and dresses him in the mornings; neither does he try alternative behaviors as an expression of his effort to accomplish the external goal of having Philip present. Despite the limitations to his reflective, goal-oriented abilities, however, Chan's change in behavior in relation to Philip's presence or absence does indicate his ability to respond to the world around him. Chan's behavior indicates that he is aware of Philip's presence or absence, and he responds accordingly.

As Buber sees it, responding to the Other we encounter as Thou, without the mediatory reflective activities of the I of I-It relations, brings forth a mutuality of helping, healing, and educating for both partners of the meeting.[76] It offers help in that it frees the Other "from their entanglement in bustling activity."[77] The Other becomes freed from the confinement of the objectifying effects of the I of I-It relations so that the Other may become real to the I, "step forth in their singleness, and confront him as Thou."[78] Jean Vanier, founder of the l'Arche communities,[79] describes well the ways in which individuals with intellectual disabilities relate to the world without the objectifying, reflective activity accessible to individuals with greater intellectual capacity:

As I grow in friendship with people who are weak and powerless, I am beginning to discover in them qualities of the heart that I find less often in people who have devoted their energies to success. . . . The people we have welcomed in L'Arche . . . have a great gift of simplicity in relationship. They are not governed by social conventions. They welcome visitors with joy, and make no distinction between those who are important in the eyes of the world and those who are not. They are not interested in anyone's profession or rank, but they are perceptive about people's hearts. They do not wear masks; they express joy and anger quite naturally. They live in the present moment, and are not caught up in a longing for the past or in dreams about the future. . . . All these qualities make men and women who welcome, celebrate and enter into relationship. Free from the urge to compete and succeed, many of them radiate joy. . . . They seem to have a greater wholeness than many people who are more intellectually or practically gifted. They show us a path of love, simplicity and joy.[80]

And as a consequence of entering into relationships with individuals with intellectual disabilities, Vanier experienced personal transformation:

They awakened a part of my being that had been under-developed, dormant. Through them, a new world began to open up for me, not the world of efficiency, competition, success and power, but the world of the heart, of vulnerability and communion. They were leading me on a path towards healing and wholeness.[81]

For Vanier, entering into communion with individuals with intellectual disabilities resulted in tremendous personal growth. Making friends with his housemates with disabilities, Raphael Simi and Philippe Seux, forced Vanier to acknowledge his own vulnerabilities and limitations. Vanier witnessed daily the reality of their pain of having experienced rejection throughout their lives. As a result, he was forced to stop being seduced by the activities that normally kept him distracted and to become aware of the pain within his own life—his competitive nature, his desire always to be right, always to succeed, and to be admired. Through relationship with individuals with intellectual disabilities, Vanier learned humility. He realized it was not possible to befriend Raphael and Philippe with love and compassion without first coming down from his own pedestal and recognizing his common humanity and vulnerability with them.[82]

I experienced transformation in my own life as well through relationship with individuals with profound intellectual disabilities. In my early years as a physical therapist, I was eager to apply the skills I had learned as a student to accomplish the goals I had set for my patients. Immediately upon interacting with individuals with intellectual and physical disabilities, however, I became acutely aware of the impatience I experienced when my own agenda conflicted with the abilities and gifts of my patients. More often than not, the individuals with whom I worked presented themselves to me with limitations and abilities that I could not foresee. This resulted in a steep learning curve for me, which included most importantly learning the values of patience, waiting and listening. Even though the individuals with whom I worked could not speak to me with words, I learned that they spoke most profoundly with their bodies. To "listen" to the bodies of these individuals was something I had to learn; it did not come quickly. I first had to learn to be patient and to wait for their bodily responses, which often took several seconds—even minutes. And I had to learn to sacrifice my own agenda as I "listened" to their bodies and learned of the gifts and abilities that were accessible to them.

Vanier speaks of a similar experience of learning to listen through befriending individuals with intellectual disabilities. He writes,

> When you are with people who suffer from mental handicaps, you cannot be in a hurry. It takes time to listen to them and understand them. Efficiency is not their strong point! . . . It is not just a question of listening to words, but also to the non-verbal, to body language. Raphael hardly spoke at all. . . . I had to learn to interpret his bodily gestures, his tears, his smiles, his touch, his cries of anger that sprang from frustration. People with mental handicaps express themselves more through their bodies than through words. We have to be very attentive to this simple, concrete language to grasp the pain and the problems as well as the desires behind it.[83]

For Vanier, the humility, the patience, and the ability to listen that he learned through relationships with individuals with intellectual disabilities resulted in a greater consistency between who he was and who he professed to be as a Christian.[84] These relationships transformed him from a man who valued success and power to a man whose life reflected more clearly the patience, humility, and compassion of Christ.

Buber speaks of such a transformation through relationship as an education in character. Through participation in relationships freed from the objectifying, categorizing functions of the I of I-It relations, we experience a growth in unity between who we are and who we profess to be. This is growth in character, for Buber—"the special link between man's being and his appearance, the special connection between the unity of what he is and the sequence of his actions and attitude."[85] Education in character does not occur in relationships in which education is the motive. It cannot take place when the Other is engaged as an object for education. Rather, character develops in relationships in which one participates with his or her whole being and with spontaneity, with no thought of how he or she will affect the Other. For one who educates others in character, "his aliveness streams out to them and affects them most strongly and purely when he has no thought of affecting them."[86] For Vanier, a transformation in character occurred in a way similar to what Buber describes here. Through relationship with individuals with intellectual disabilities, who engaged him fully and spontaneously, with no ulterior motive of transforming his character, Vanier received an education in the values of patience, humility, and listening.

Buber's point in discussing the ways in which helping, healing, and educating occur in I-Thou relations is not that such effects occur in a unidirectional way. The effects of participating in relationships freed from objectification of the Other are shared mutually by both partners in the meeting. For Vanier, the impact of relating with individuals with intellectual disabilities reached beyond his own transformation. Through participation in relationships in which they were loved and accepted as they are, often for the first time, many individuals with intellectual disabilities at l'Arche demonstrated a change in their behavior away from what appeared as anger and withdrawal to behavior that indicated a growth in peacefulness and joy.[87] The mutuality of the effects of helping, healing, and educating of which Buber speaks extends beyond the experience of the able-minded to include offering help and healing to individuals with intellectual disabilities as well.

Buber speaks of the mutuality of the effects of the I-Thou relation not only in terms of bringing help and education to the partners of the meeting. He speaks as well of mutuality in terms of reciprocal constitution of the I and Thou—"human being becomes an I on account of the Thou."[88] This means for Buber that both I and Thou find their existence as human beings as a result of responding to one another with the totality, immediacy, grace, and will characteristic of the I-Thou relation.[89] For Buber, it is essential to being human that we respond to the Other we encounter as Thou. As mentioned earlier, however, Buber's claim that human being becomes an I on account of the Thou includes the constitution of the dialogue partners not only through responding to one another as Thou, but also through being addressed as Thou. I become not only through responding to my Other as Thou, but also because she addresses me as Thou. For Buber, this "being addressed" can be performed by objects in nature, as in the "grace" that is offered by a tree as "bodied over against me," or it can be performed by a human being who approaches us as we go our own way.[90] The point here is that, for Buber, the humanity of the partners in dialogue is constituted reciprocally both as they respond to one another without the reflective, categorizing functions of the I of I-It relations, and as they are addressed by one another in the same way.[91]

How this mutual effect of constitution of the self through the dialogical, address-response character of the I-Thou relation relates to individuals with profound intellectual disabilities like Chan should be evident by now. We have noted the numerous ways in which Chan's behavior demonstrates his responsiveness to the world around him— the changes in his behavioral state in response to the presence of others, the changes in his muscle tone in response to changes in the position of his body and changes in his external environment. The many ways in which Chan responds to the world around him, and yet without behavior that indicates reflective, objectifying engagement, signals Chan's ability to encounter objects in his environment in ways characteristic of the I-Thou encounter which Buber describes. And given Buber's anthropology, Chan's behavior signals his humanity as one who responds to the beings he encounters in nonobjectifying ways.

With regard to the constitution of the self through being addressed as Thou, individuals like Chan acquire their humanity insofar as they are approached as Thou by the Thou they encounter. Given Buber's anthropology, Chan would be considered human not only because he was responsive to the world around him, without the perspectival functions of the I of I-It relations, but also because he was addressed as Thou by the Thou he encounters. To the degree that Chan is engaged without becoming an object of the needs of the Other whom he encounters, he would be seen as human being.

Buber's idea that one's identity as human being is reciprocally constituted through participation in I-Thou relations has obvious implications for the development of an ethic of care for individuals with profound intellectual disabilities. To reconceive the concept no longer in terms of those with the intellectual capacity for moral reasoning, freedom of choice, and so forth, but, as Buber conceives it, in terms of those who are responsive to the world without objectifying it, opens up the concept to include a much wider population of beings, including not only individuals with profound intellectual disabilities but also all beings with the capacity for responsiveness. Assuming that the word "human being" names that which is valuable to the degree that it is deserving of care and protection from harm, reconceiving "human being" in this way serves as grounds for condemnation of the neglect and outright abuse that has often been inflicted upon individuals with profound intellectual disabilities in the institutions that house them and calls for the development of public policy ensuring that they receive the care and freedom from harm that is expected on behalf of those without intellectual disabilities.

Buber's reconception of "human being" to include the constitution of the self through being addressed as Thou, and not only as a result of the capacity for responsiveness without objectification, also names the impact of our actions toward individuals with profound intellectual disabilities, and all beings. It acknowledges the power that individuals with higher levels of intellectual functioning possess—in Buber's terms, the ability to choose to address the Other as It or as Thou. It is "the melancholy of our fate," Buber claims, that those with the ability to do so will eventually objectify that which they encounter.[92] To acknowledge this power is to name the responsibility that individuals with higher intellectual functioning have to address as Thou the beings they encounter, lest they dehumanize them. And the irony here, given Buber's anthropology, is that the attitude we take toward the Other we encounter will impact not only the humanity of the Other but also our own. Whether we respond to the Other as It or as Thou determines our own humanity, for Buber, insofar as personhood or "human being" involves engaging the Other freed from one's own perspectival needs.[93]

In this chapter, I have attempted an anthropological interpretation of the phenomenology of the relationality of Chan provided in Chapter 3. Given Chan's responsiveness to the world around him, I have attempted to demonstrate the ways in which his behavior is expressive of his humanity, as Buber understands the term. For Buber, human existence is not found through participation in I-It relations in which the I engages the Other from the perspective of its own needs, wants, and interests. Rather, human existence is to be found through participation in I-Thou relations, which Buber characterizes as involving immediacy, totalization, the coming together of will and grace, and mutuality. Using the description of Chan's behavior from Chapter 3, I have tried to indicate that these qualities are accessible to individuals with profound intellectual disabilities like Chan, whose behavior expresses the ability to engage the world around him without the perspectival functions of the I of I-It relations. I have argued that reconceiving "human being" in ways similar to Buber's approach opens up the possibility of recognizing the full humanity of individuals with profound intellectual disabilities like Chan, thereby calling for public policy that would mandate their humane treatment. I have also argued that reconceiving "human being" in this way acknowledges the responsibility that individuals who possess the ability to engage the world reflectively have to respond to the Other with intellectual disabilities in humanizing, nonobjectifying ways.

In the next chapter, I discuss the relevance of this alternative anthropology for theology. I respond to the questions of what it means to be human in the eyes of God and what it means to experience God. Again with Buber's help, I suggest that the *imago Dei* has little to do with what capacity one may or may not possess. Rather, I suggest that that which reflects the *imago Dei* participates in relationships of responsiveness to the world in nonobjectifying, utilitarian ways. Similarly, I suggest that what it means to experience God is not limited to those with the ability to comprehend comprehensive conceptual schemes. To experience God is also to participate in these relationships.

5. *Imago Dei* as Rationality or Relationality: History and Construction

WHEN THROUGHOUT THE CENTURIES Christians have had questions about the meaning of human life, they have turned to a concept, traditionally rendered in Latin: the *imago Dei*. The term comes from the Hebrew scriptures and indicates that humanity in the intention of God is humanity "in the image of God."[1] The origins of the *imago Dei* symbol are found in the book of Genesis in only three direct references. The first reference is found in Genesis 1:26–27, in which the priestly writer, "P," offers an account of the creation of the world:

> Then God said: "Let us make humankind in our image, after our likeness; and let them have dominion over the fish of the sea, and over the birds of the air, and over the cattle, and over all the earth, and over every creeping thing that creeps on the earth." (27) So God created humankind in God's own image, in the image of God God created humankind; male and female God created them. (28) And God blessed them, and God said to them, "Be fruitful and multiply, and fill the earth and subdue it; and have dominion over the fish of the sea and over the birds of the air and over every living thing that moves upon the earth." (RSV)

The second reference dealing with the image of God is Genesis 5:1–3:

> This is the book of the generations of Adam. When God created humankind, God made humankind in the likeness of God. (2) Male and female God created them, and God blessed them and named them humankind when they were created. (3) When Adam had lived a hundred and thirty years, he became the father of a son in his own likeness, after his image, and named him Seth. (RSV)

The final reference, Genesis 9:5–6, follows the story of the great flood and locates the value of human life in its being created in the image of God:

> God said to Noah: "For your lifeblood I will surely require a reckoning; of every beast I will require it and of humankind; of every human being's brother I will require the life of human being. Whoever sheds the blood of human being, by human being shall his blood be shed; for God made human being in God's own image." (NSV)

There are a variety of interpretations of the meaning of this symbol as it appears in the Hebrew scriptures. It has been argued, for example, that the symbol indicates a physical resemblance between the human being and God. According to Cuthbert A. Simpson, "In the mind of P, there can be little doubt, bodily form was to some extent at any rate involved in the idea of the divine image."[2] It has been argued as well that the symbol of the *imago Dei* is linked with the idea that human beings have dominion over other creatures. This argument is often based on the symbol as it is found in Genesis 1:26, "Let us make humankind in our image, after our likeness, and let them have dominion over the fish of the sea, and over the birds of the air, and over the cattle . . ." Critics of this interpretation of the *imago Dei* symbol have argued that mere proximity between the *imago* and *dominium* does not necessitate equating the two concepts.[3] Still others have argued that it would be irresponsible exegetically to dissociate the *imago Dei* symbol entirely from the concept of human dominion, though it would be necessary to understand this "dominion" as an expression of the long-suffering love of God and not the abusive dominion of a despot.[4]

Paul Ramsey offers a helpful rubric for understanding the variety of interpretations of the *imago Dei* symbol. He divides them into two categories: the substantialist conception and the relational conception.[5] The substantialist conception considers the *imago Dei* as referring to the human being's possessing some quality, capacity, or characteristic inherent in its creaturely substance that renders it similar to God.[6] In Ramsey's words, a substantialist conception of the *imago Dei* symbol refers to "something within the substantial form of human nature, some faculty or capacity man possesses" that distinguishes "man from nature and from other animals."[7]

There are a number of problems with this approach to understanding the *imago Dei* symbol. An obvious one is the tendency to consider the possession of that quality or capacity which distinguishes human beings from the rest of creation as an attribution to human being of superior status when compared to those beings who do not possess it. As Douglas John Hall writes, "It is hardly possible to adopt the kind of inherently comparative language involved in this approach without placing strong value judgments on the characteristics that are singled out as constituting the locus of the *imago* in the human creature."[8] And because in the history of the *imago Dei* theology what distinguished human being from the rest of creation was often a characteristic that transcends our physical nature, including especially our "spiritual" or intellectual nature, the result has been the devaluation and often abuse of animals and inanimate objects—and those individuals with profound intellectual disabilities.

Another problem with substantialist efforts to identify the *imago Dei* symbol with a particular capacity or quality is the tendency by Christian theologians to valorize those qualities esteemed in the society to which they belong. As Hendrikus Berkhof has observed, "By studying how systematic theologies have poured meaning into Genesis 1:26, one could write a piece of Europe's cultural history."[9] One has only to think here of Kant's moral imperative and its expression in those nineteenth- and twentieth-century theologies that emphasize a sense of moral obligation as the quality distinguishing human being from the rest of creation. This tendency to identify the *imago Dei* with the values prevalent in a particular culture may lead to the unfortunate consequence that the Christian community has no distinctive image of the human by which to critique existing social biases.[10]

An alternative to the substantialist interpretation of the *imago Dei* symbol in the history of Christian theology has been what Ramsey refers to as the relational conception. This conception presupposes the relationship between Creator and creature, and it considers the image of God to be something that occurs as a result of this relationship. Here the *imago Dei* symbol does not indicate possessing something, but rather being or doing something. It indicates participation in relationship with God.[11] An example of a relational conception of the *imago Dei* symbol is Martin Luther's notion that the image of God is determined by the response of human beings to God.[12] For Luther, the image of God is dependent on an ongoing response of faith and trust in God and not on the possession of some quality or capacity. Thus, there is no "remnant" of the image in humanity that has "fallen" or damaged its relationship with God. There is no quality or capacity inherent in human being that continues to reflect God's image once the relationship with God has been interrupted. Rather, for Luther, the image of God that was the consequence of this relationship is "lost" and only a response of faith in God can retrieve it.[13]

There are difficulties with the relational interpretation of the *imago Dei* symbol as well, especially as Luther conceives it. Although the emphasis on a capacity is diminished here in favor of the relationship between Creator and creature, it could still be argued that a substantialist tendency remains, since the requisite participation in relationship with God requires the intellectual ability to believe in the existence of God and trust in the faithfulness and goodness of God. In addition, those relational conceptions that, like Luther's, emphasize the response of faithfulness to God are inconsistent with those references in Genesis that indicate the presence of the image in all human beings, regardless and even in spite of the nature of their responsiveness to God.

THOMAS AQUINAS ON THE *IMAGO DEI*

An example of the substantialist conception of the *imago Dei* symbol is Thomas Aquinas's understanding of human reason as the seat of the image of God. In Question 93 of *Summa Theologica*, Thomas Aquinas discusses at length the image of God as it is expressed in human intellectual capacity. He claims first that the image of God is found in human beings, and he grounds this claim in the words of the priestly author of Genesis 1:26, "Let us make human being to Our own image and likeness." He then claims that only intellectual creatures properly image God, and he defends this claim based on the degree to which intellectual creatures approach God's likeness:

> Some things are like God first and most commonly because they exist; secondly, because they live; and thirdly because they know or understand; and these last, as Augustine says, 'approach so near to God in likeness, that among all creatures nothing comes nearer to Him.' It is clear, therefore, that intellectual creatures alone, properly speaking, are made to God's image.[14]

While all creatures bear the likeness of God, only intellectual creatures "properly" image God because they approach God's likeness to a very high degree due to their capacity for knowledge and understanding.

Although Aquinas maintains that only intellectual creatures "properly" image God, he does not believe that creatures without intellectual capacities utterly lack the image of God. Certainly there is evidence in the *Summa* that Aquinas takes such an exclusive position. He writes, "Augustine says: 'Man's excellence consists in the fact that God made him to his own image by giving him an intellectual mind, which raises him above the beasts of the field.' Therefore things without intellect are not made to God's image."[15] Aquinas appears here to deny the image of God to any creature lacking intellectual ability. Further investigation, however, reveals that Aquinas nuances this position. He later claims that, although only intellectual creatures approach the likeness of God to the point of "properly" bearing God's image, even those creatures that fall short of the image of God participate to some degree in the image because they bear to some degree a likeness to God. Aquinas's position on what participates in God's image, therefore, is not as exclusive as some passages may indicate, given his position on the expression of that image in all that bears a likeness to God.

Although Aquinas broadens the concept of the *imago Dei* to include some level of participation in it by those creatures lacking in intellectual ability, he still believes that only intellectual creatures "properly" image God. By that we take him to mean that, because they possess the ability to know or understand, only intellectual creatures bear the likeness of God to the degree that none other comes nearer to God so as to bear God's image "properly."[16] But what exactly does Aquinas mean by "the ability to know or understand," and why is this ability necessary for one to bear the image of God properly?

In Article 4 of Question 93, Aquinas clarifies what he means by the ability of intellectual creatures "to know or understand," and he clarifies why this ability is significant as an indicator of those who "properly" bear the image of God. He states that only human beings properly image God because only they are able to imitate God in God's ability to understand and love God's self.[17] Thus, the ability "to know or understand" involves the ability to understand and love God. And this ability to know and love God indicates a "proper" image-bearer of God because only individuals with this ability are able to imitate God in God's ability to know and love God's self. Only intellectual creatures "properly" image God because only they are able to participate in God's ability to understand and love God's self. They are able to do this in three ways:

> First, because man possesses a natural aptitude for understanding and loving God; and this aptitude consists in the very nature of the mind, which is common to all men. Secondly, because man actually or habitually knows and loves God, though imperfectly; and this image consists in the conformity of grace. Thirdly, because man knows and loves God perfectly; and this image consists in the likeness of glory.[18]

We see from this passage that for Aquinas all human beings bear this image, though not necessarily with equal brightness.[19] The image of God is found in our natural power or aptitude for knowing and loving God. This comes as a gift to all human beings, because all human beings possess a mind.[20] There is the image of God that is found, albeit imperfectly, in all believers as they actually or habitually know and love God. And there is the image of God that is found only in those who, because they have entered into glory, actually know and love God perfectly. The important point here is that in each mode of expression of the image of God, whether in aptitude or actuality, the intellectual ability to imitate God in God's ability to understand and love God is emphasized.

Aquinas gives further support for his position that only intellectual creatures are proper image-bearers of God by way of his claim that the image of God is more in angels than in human beings. Aquinas claims that because the image of God consists chiefly in the intellectual nature, and because the intellectual nature in angels is more perfect than in human beings, angels are more in the image of God than human beings. Granted, the image of God exists in human beings in secondary ways. For example, human beings imitate God because human being proceeds from human being, just as God proceeds from God. The entire human soul is in the entire human body as well, just as God is in regard to the entire world.[21] In these things, according to Aquinas, one could say that the image of God is more perfect in human beings than it is in angels; but, he writes, "These do not of themselves belong to the notion of the Divine image in human being."[22] As we explore each aspect of Aquinas's argument regarding what makes a being a "proper" image-bearer of God, his emphasis on intellectual ability becomes ever more transparent. Only those creatures with an intellectual nature "properly" image God, because only they possess the ability to imitate God in God's ability to understand and love God's self.

The obvious question here in relation to individuals with profound intellectual abilities is this: In what way might these individuals be image bearers, given Aquinas's view of the *imago Dei*? In what way might individuals with profound intellectual disabilities be considered to bear God's image "properly," given that their behavior indicates that they lack the ability to employ the concepts of self and other necessary for reflection upon that which exists beyond themselves? In Chan's case, his behavior indicates that he does not have the ability to symbolize the self as distinct from the other necessary to conceive of a goal and to act with the intent to achieve it. Chan's attempt to right himself in midline in response to Sarah's positioning him out of midline does not intensify when he is unsuccessful; neither does he try an alternative method (such as reaching for Sara's arms) as an indication of his awareness that he is sitting out of midline or of his goal of returning to midline. Nor does he alternate his gaze between Sara and the location of a midline sitting position as if to communicate to her his desire to sit upright. Given that Chan's behavior does not indicate the ability to conceive of himself as a self distinct from the world around him, it is difficult to regard Chan as an image bearer of God on Aquinas's terms. It is difficult to conceive of Chan as possessing the requisite intellectual capacity for understanding and loving God, given what appears to be an inability to employ the concepts of self and other necessary for reflection on that which exists outside the self.

JOHN CALVIN ON THE *IMAGO DEI*

Whereas the substantialistic conception of the *imago Dei* locates the image in the possession of a particular capacity, quality, or endowment, a relational conception of the *imago Dei* conceives of the image not as something possessed but something enacted—that is, turning toward God. An example of such a relational conception of the *imago Dei* is John Calvin's understanding of the image as obediently reflecting God's will in one's life. For Calvin, the proper seat of the image of God is in the soul, which he considers primarily in terms of our intellectual capacities. He finds evidence for the soul through "the many preeminent gifts with which the human mind is endowed" and "the nimbleness of the human mind in searching out heaven and earth and the secrets of nature . . . in arranging each thing in its proper order, and in inferring future events from the past."[23] He finds evidence for the soul as well in that "with our intelligence we conceive the invisible God and the angels, something the body can by no means do. We grasp things that are right, just and honorable, which are hidden to the bodily senses."[24] Clearly, Calvin's intellectualist understanding of the soul combined with his understanding of the soul as the "proper" seat of the image of God is problematic when one considers ways in which individuals with profound intellectual disabilities bear this image.

Like Aquinas, Calvin claims that the image of God can be found in all of creation. Just as God from moment to moment sustains the universe in being, the universe from moment to moment images the glory of God.[25] In his commentary on Psalm 19 ("The heavens are telling the glory of God"), he writes,

> There is certainly nothing so obscure or contemptible, even in the
> smallest corners of the earth, in which some marks of the power and

wisdom of God may not be seen; but as a more distinct image of him is engraven on the heavens, David has particularly selected them for contemplation.[26]

Thus, all things bear the image of God for Calvin, and yet there is a special sense for him in which human beings image God:

> It is certain that in every part of the world some lineaments of divine glory are beheld, and hence we may infer that when his image is placed in man, there is a kind of antithesis, as it were, setting man apart from the crowd, and exalting him above all the other creatures.[27]

The question here becomes: In what way for Calvin do human beings bear the image of God? According to Douglas John Hall, Calvin avoids the conventional answer that identifies the *imago Dei* in human beings with some capacity, characteristic, or endowment they innately possess.[28] For example, Calvin denies Augustine's efforts to identify the *imago Dei* with the three faculties of the soul: the intellect, the memory, and the will. He writes, "I have no difficulty in admitting the above distinction of the faculties of the soul . . . but a definition of the image of God ought to rest on a firmer basis than such subtleties."[29] He also rejects the position of "the Anthropomorphites," who "were too gross in seeking this resemblance in the body,"[30] as well as the interpretation of those who locate "the similitude of God" in "the dominion committed to man; as though he resembled God only in this character, that he was constituted heir and possessor of all things."[31]

Thus, Calvin rejects identifying the *imago Dei* in human being with a particular aspect of human nature, such as a quality or characteristic. For him, the *imago Dei* deals more with what human beings do than with what they possess. It has to do with the orientation of human beings in relation to their Creator—that of reflecting God's glory back to God through obedience in relation to God. As Calvin writes in his sermon on Deuteronomy 4:10,

> God created us after his own image in order that his truth might shine forth in us. It is not God's purpose that men should abolish and destroy the grace that he has put in them, for that would be utterly to

deface his image in spite of him, but rather, that as he comes nearer to us and we to him, so he will have his image known in us, and his truth shine forth in us all the more. Let us understand that it is not the intention of God that we should be ignorant of him, but to utter himself in such a way, that we may be able to distinguish him from forged idols, that we may take him for our Father, and assure ourselves that we are called to the knowledge of the truth, and that we may boldly resort to him to call upon him and seek succour at his hand.[32]

Thus, while it is true for Calvin that all creatures bear the image of God, human beings reflect God's glory in a special way. Inanimate creatures and creatures without reason do this unconsciously; they image God in that through their splendor, complexity, and beauty we witness the glory of God.[33] Human beings, on the other hand, reflect God when they consciously acknowledge their dependence on God and give God their obedience.[34]

This brings us to a central metaphor in Calvin's understanding of human beings as image bearers of God: the mirror. For Calvin, the vocation of human beings is to mirror or to reflect the glory of God from a position within creation.[35] In his words, human beings "ought to be accounted a mirror of the Divine glory."[36] According to Hall, the significance of this metaphor in Calvin's interpretation of the *imago Dei* in human beings is that it precludes understanding it as an endowment or capacity.[37] "Only while the mirror actually reflects an object does it have the image of that object. There is no such thing in Calvin's thought as an imago dissociated from the act of reflecting."[38] Thus, when Calvin refers to the image of God in Adam in terms of his possession of "right understanding," he is not speaking of the capacity for understanding as the location of the imago. Rather, he is presupposing something about the orientation of the creature in relation to the Creator. He speaks of the imago as

the integrity which Adam possessed, when he was endued with a right understanding . . . when he had affections regulated by reason, and all his senses governed in proper order, and when, in the excellency of his nature, he truly resembled the excellence of his

Creator. And though the principle seat of the Divine image was in the mind and heart or in the soul and its faculties, yet there was no part of man, not even the body, which was not adorned with some rays of its glory.[39]

Calvin is not indicating here that the *imago Dei* is to be identified with the human capacity for understanding or reasoning. Rather, he is indicating that human beings reflect or mirror the glory of God, with right understanding and properly ordered senses and affections, when in relation to God they respond to God's presence with obedience.[40]

It is important to note here that it is not merely in the mirroring or reflecting that human beings image God, for Calvin, since what a mirror images is dependent upon what the mirror is turned toward. If the "mirror" turns away from God and toward the quest for satisfaction in things, it exchanges the image of God for the image of something else.[41] Rather, the image of God consists in the position of the human being before God. It exists in human beings as they consciously and obediently turn toward God in such a way that God may be able to behold God's self in human beings as in a mirror.[42] Paul Ramsey offers the following interpretation of Calvin's view of the *imago* in human being and writes,

> The image of God is . . . to be understood as a relationship within which man sometimes stands, whenever like a mirror he obediently reflects God's will in his life and actions. . . . Nothing about man not presently involved in response to God can be called God's image. The mirror itself is not the image; the mirror images; God's image is in the mirror. The image of God, according to this view, consists of man's position before God, or, rather, the image of God is reflected in man because of his position before him.[43]

Thus, for Calvin, when human beings turn toward God and respond obediently to God's will, the image of God is reflected in them, but when they turn away from God, they lose certain qualities that pertain to relationship with God.[44] Only in the act of responding obediently in relation to God is the image of God reflected or mirrored in human being.

Calvin's relational understanding of the *imago Dei* in human being has its salutary aspects. For example, it protects the concept of sin as estrangement from God—a concept that becomes problematic with the substantialist notion that there is some remnant of the image of God in human being even after the "fall" of the relationship with God. For evangelical theologians in particular, this understanding of sin is significant as it acknowledges our utter depravity in relationship to God which results from our disobedience to God's call for our faithful response, and it acknowledges the loss of relationship with God that can be restored only by grace through faith. For evangelicals, Calvin's understanding of the image of God in relational terms, as the reflection of God's glory as one obediently chooses God's will in one's life and actions, is indispensable to Christian faith inasmuch as it allows us to acknowledge the responsibility that human beings have in their relationship to God.

Despite the advantages of Calvin's relational understanding of the *imago Dei* in human beings, significant for our purposes is the question of whether Calvin has in fact avoided the pitfalls of a substantialist theological anthropology. Has Calvin avoided the substantialist tendency to locate the *imago Dei* in a capacity or quality innate to human beings, or is there a remnant of substantialist thinking in his theology of human being? Granted, there is evidence that Calvin attempts to avoid substantialist thinking as he rejects the location of the *imago Dei* in the faculties of the soul, in the body, or in the capacity for dominion over the rest of creation. But as I see it, he does not succeed in full, because Calvin takes for granted that obedient response to God requires the intellectual ability to understand the commands or wishes of God, as well as the ability and thereby the freedom to disobey them. For Calvin, it is for these activities that we have been given the gift of reason.[45] But if reason is required to perform the activities that mirror God's image in us—if reason is required in order for human being to understand God's commandments and respond obediently to them—then a substantialist tendency remains in Calvin's anthropology. Despite his efforts to conceive of the *imago Dei* in human being in relational terms, Calvin employs a substantialist move by claiming that the *imago Dei* involves responding obediently to God's commands, because it requires the intellectual ability to conceive of God's commands and intentionally choose to obey them. We have already noted the difficulties with such a substantialist position, given the inability of individuals like Chan to symbolize self and other necessary for intentional, goal-directed behavior. Thus, Calvin privileges intellectual ability in his understanding of the *imago Dei*, and that becomes problematic because it automatically excludes individuals with profound intellectual disabilities from participation in the image of God.

Again, it is not that I find Calvin's understanding of the image of God in human being lacking in salutary aspects altogether. In fact, I find his use of the "mirror" metaphor helpful, as long as we understand what mirrors God to include not only responsiveness to God in the form of understanding God's commands and self-conscious obedience to them but also responsiveness to the world around us in less cognitive, nonsymbolic ways. Rather, the aspect of Calvin's conception of the image of God in human being that I seek to avoid is his persistent emphasis on the intellectual aspect to that which mirrors God in human being.

THE *IMAGO DEI* AS PARTICIPATION IN RELATIONSHIPS OF MUTUAL RESPONSIVENESS

Over against the substantialist tendency to privilege intellectual ability in both Aquinas's and Calvin's conceptions of the *imago Dei* in human being, I suggest an alternative understanding of the *imago Dei* that avoids the emphasis on a capacity or quality, intellectual or otherwise, and emphasizes instead mutual responsiveness. Being an image bearer of God is not limited to a particular capacity. Rather, I argue, the *imago Dei* in human being is a relational concept that involves participation in the meeting between responsive partners.

Such responsiveness would certainly include the capacity of language users to communicate to one another with ideas, concepts, feelings, and so on. I do not deny that verbal and intellectual interaction may provide greater depth and complexity in human relationships of mutual love and responsiveness. Such responsiveness would also include the capacity for symbolization that is required for intentional agency. I do not deny that the capacity to engage symbols of self and other allow an individual to respond to the world with purpose and intentionality. I do not intend to leave behind the capacities for intentionality, symbolization, and linguisticality. Rather, I am resisting those theological anthropologies that locate human being in the possession of a particular capacity, as in Kaufman's emphasis on the capacities for symbolization and intentional agency or Lindbeck's emphasis on symbolic, linguistic ability. And I am resisting those theological anthropologies that locate the *imago Dei* in human being in a particular capacity, as in Aquinas's emphasis on the intellectual capacity to understand and love God or Calvin's emphasis on the gift of reason as necessary to respond with obedience to God's commandments.

I am suggesting instead that what it means to image God has to do with one's participation in relationships as responders, which includes not only responsiveness that employs symbolic material but also nonsymbolic modes of responsiveness. With my phenomenological description of Chan's behavior, I have attempted to demonstrate the ways in which this nonsymbolic responsiveness is possible. Chan responds, albeit nonsymbolically, to the world around him. His behavioral state changes in response to Philip's presence: He demonstrates more "awake behavior" as the motor activity of his arms and legs increases, his eyes remain open, he smiles and begins to vocalize at the sound of Philip's voice, and he demonstrates less "awake behavior" when another caregiver enters his room. The important point, as I indicated earlier, is that Chan's responsiveness indicates none of the behavioral criteria of intentional communication. He does not change the signal quality until the goal has been met, that is, the sleep behavior does not intensify if Philip leaves the room, as an attempt to accomplish the goal of communicating his desire for Philip to remain present. Nor does his sleep behavior cease after the other caregivers have left the room, as an indication of his awareness that the goal of Philip's presence was not met. Clearly, Chan is not responding to the world around him by using referential words or the construction of linguistic propositions. Nor is there evidence that Chan uses preverbal gestures with intent to communicate a want or need. Despite the lack of evidence that Chan employs symbols of self and other as he responds to Philip or the other caregivers, Chan does respond to the world around him through changes in his behavior, and the world in turn responds to him. And these changes in Chan's behavior appear to serve a communicative function not because they are an intentional attempt by Chan to communicate but because they are interpreted by those language users around him as expressive of wants and needs of which Chan appears to be unaware. Chan's responsiveness to the world around him without the use of symbolic material serves as evidence of the need for the theological anthropology that I am proposing in which the *imago Dei* in human being is understood in terms of participation in relationships of mutual responsiveness, whether symbolic or non-symbolic, and not in terms of the possession of a particular, "essential" capacity, such as the intellectual ability to employ signs and symbols for intentional communication or intentional agency of any kind.

GOD AS YEARNING

It is important at this point to indicate what I mean with my use of the concept "God." Any claim about what it means to image God implies a theology of God, and my claim that imaging God includes participation in nonsymbolic, mutually responsive relations is no exception. There are two primary resources on which I draw in my understanding of God, especially as it relates to the anthropology I have discussed earlier. The first resource is the Hebrew Bible, in which God is portrayed in anthropomorphic terms as the creator and sustainer of the world. Here God's desire to be in relationship with human beings is expressed initially through the story of God's relationship with Adam and Eve. Through God's creation of the first human beings, God is portrayed as desiring relationship with humanity. Despite the disobedience of Adam and Eve to God's offer of relationship with them, God's desire for relationship continues as the history of salvation unfolds through a number of covenants God makes with God's people. Through these covenants, God promises to be faithful to God's people whether they accept or reject God's love.

There are stories throughout the Hebrew Bible of Israel's waning trust in God in the face of adversity and God's response of longsuffering and faithfulness to her. I am reminded in particular of the story in the book of Exodus in which the people of Israel complain to Moses in the wilderness because they are thirsty and have no water to drink.[46] Moses cried to God, and God responded by bringing water to Israel. God is said to have named the place of Israel's faithlessness "Massah" and "Meribah," from the Hebrew verbs "test" and "find fault." Despite Israel's weakness of faith in the midst of adversity, God responds to her complaints with faithfulness to her and the provision of her needs. The Hebrew Bible is rife with similar stories indicating God's responsiveness to Israel and her responsiveness to God. Such stories portray God not in deistic terms as removed from the concerns of the world God created. Rather, God is portrayed as intimately involved with God's creation, responsive to the concerns of God's people and desirous of relationship with them. It is this God portrayed in the Hebrew Bible that initially informs my understanding of God as participating in relationships of mutual responsiveness with God's people.

While I find these biblical stories a helpful resource for conceiving of God as a participant in responsive relationships, there are limits to anthropomorphizing discourse. Kaufman himself indicates the problems with conceiving of God in this way. He speaks of the dualism between God and the world that results from an understanding of God as a quasi-human agent who created the world and continues to care for it. God is conceived here as somehow "outside" or "other than" the world, just as human potters are outside and other than the pots they create.[47] This dualism is no longer plausible for many who possess a modern concept of the universe. For these people, the universe is all there is. In what way could they speak of something "outside" it?[48] This dualism is also problematic because it portrays God as the distinct being who is both desirous of relationship with us as well the object of our desire. As I will discuss, this difficulty with a dualistic view of the God/world relation is especially problematic when one considers ways in which individuals with profound intellectual disabilities participate in the image of God. Kaufman notes other problems with this conception of God. Understanding God as an all-powerful cosmic agent may lead to the notion of God as an authoritarian tyrant, "one who is arbitrary and unjust in the exercise of omnipotence."[49]

Conceiving of God in this way has often led to the drive toward domination and control in the history of the Christian tradition. Believers have often taken this God of unquestionable authority as authorizing destructive human activities, such as "holy wars, inquisitions, and torture."[50]

My point here is not to indicate that the conception of God in anthropomorphic terms as a human wholly problematic. In fact, such humanization of God serves the valuable function of provoking a powerful affective response from religious practitioners—to love God, to serve God, to trust God regardless of life's circumstances.[51] This conception of God brings to human life an understanding of what is meaningful and valuable, which human beings then use to bring order to their lives. My point, rather, is to indicate that despite the value such a conception of God brings to human life, there are problems with this conception that may result in more harm than good.

Thus, I find an additional resource necessary for understanding God in a way that is mindful of God as a participant in relationship and yet without the pitfalls of anthropomorphizing God. I turn to the works of Pseudo-Dionysius here, in particular *The Divine Names*, in which God is portrayed as both yearning itself and the object of that yearning. Occasionally Pseudo-Dionysius personifies God to make his point. He uses courtly imagery and refers to God as both the lover who yearns for the Beloved as well as the Beloved who is the object of that yearning. It is not the case for Pseudo-Dionysius that God is somehow a person with the intellectual capacity to conceive of the other as the distinct being whom God desires. Rather, God is portrayed here as yearning itself, as well as that which is yearned for. God both produces or generates the yearning and is the object of that yearning. God is yearning and love because God is the power that moves all things up to God's self, and God is the yearned-for and the beloved because God is beautiful and good. For Pseudo-Dionysius, this divine yearning brings a unity, a commingling, or an ecstasy so that the lover belongs no longer to the self but to the beloved. Dionysius notes a number of biblical references that support this understanding of the unifying nature of the divine yearning. For instance, he cites Paul's yearning for God as an example of the unifying power of the divine yearning. He explains this is why Paul was inspired to write these words to the

Galatians: "It is no longer I who live, but Christ who lives in me."[52] To cite Paul in his second letter to the Corinthians, Dionysius states that Paul was beside himself for God, "possessing not his own life but the life of the One for whom he yearned."[53] The result here is not a conceptual separation between the yearning and the yearned-for, but rather the unbeginning and unending nature of the divine yearning as traveling "through the Good, from the Good, in the Good and to the Good . . . ever in the same direction, always proceeding, always remaining, always being restored to itself."[54]

Pseudo-Dionysius's thought here is helpful for my purposes because it provides a way of thematizing God without conceptualization. His idea of God as yearning itself avoids the pitfalls of locating this desire in the intellect, including the dualism between the yearning bodies and the divine itself that results when God is conceived as the object of our yearning. God conceived in this way—as extrinsic to the world—cannot be encountered in the world by those with profound intellectual disabilities. Pseudo-Dionysius's concept of God, however, focuses on the idea of yearning as both bodily and divine thereby providing a way of speaking of individuals like Chan as being part of the divine life. If with Dionysius we conceive of God in bodily terms as longing itself, rather than in intellectual terms as the object of longing, then we have the conceptual space to include the ways in which Chan's body testifies to this longing as expressive of God.

I am thinking in particular here of Chan's behavior as he responds to Philip's presence or absence. He demonstrates more awake behavior with Philip's presence and more sleep behavior with Philip's absence. Although Chan's behavior does not demonstrate the ability to conceive of Philip as the object of his desire—that is, his sleep behavior does not intensify if Philip remains absent in an effort to communicate his desire for Philip's presence—his behavior does appear to be expressive of wants and needs of which Chan is unaware. I am thinking as well of Chan's behavior as he responds to the game of volley taking place at the day treatment center. Chan begins to vocalize, and the motor activity of his arms and legs increases. Philip interprets this behavior to mean that Chan is interested in the game and moves his wheelchair to a position from which he can participate. Although his behavior does not demonstrate the ability to conceive of the game of volley as the object of his desire—his vocalizations and motor activity do not increase as a result of a delay in Philip's response in an effort to communicate his desire to participate in the game—Philip interprets Chan's behavior as expressive of an interest in the game of which Chan is unaware.

The significant point here is that while Chan's behavior does not demonstrate an ability to conceive of the world around him as the object of his desire, his behavior does indicate a responsiveness to and relationship with the world around him which could be expressive of the nonconceptual desire of which Pseudo-Dionysius writes. And if with Pseudo-Dionysius we conceive of God in terms of yearning itself, rather than in intellectual terms as the object of yearning, then it becomes possible to understand individuals without the intellectual ability to conceive of God as the object of desire as participants in the image of God. These individuals image God not because of some intellectual capacity they possess, but because their participation as responders in relationships is expressive of the longing that God is.

Having discussed the concept of God that grounds my understanding of the human, let me return to my theological anthropology and address some questions that may arise for the reader. One may sense that I am appealing to essentialism with my alternative theological anthropology, since it requires the ability to respond to the world, either symbolically or nonsymbolically.

I have two comments here. First, if there is an essentialism here, it is not an absolute one. I am not attempting to make a statement about the image of God in human being that is final and closed to debate. Rather, I am suggesting that we acknowledge the discriminatory nature of those theological anthropologies that locate the *imago Dei* in a particular intellectual capacity, and I am suggesting that we consider an alternative anthropology that is mindful of the full humanity of individuals with profound intellectual disabilities. Such an anthropology serves a strategic function, for it seeks to acknowledge the full humanity of those individuals who have traditionally been discriminated against by appeal to other views of human being. As such, my claims about human being are open to debate as the awareness of other human situations arise that may challenge these claims and call for a different anthropology with its own unique strategic purposes.

Second, while it is true that responsiveness is central to the alternative theological anthropology I am proposing, it is important to note that this responsiveness is not possible without the other to whom one responds. To image God, I argue, is to participate in relationships of mutual responsiveness. Thus, while the ability to respond to an other is required, it is not possible to participate in the image of God without a partner to whom one responds. To image God is to respond to an other in a variety of ways, intellectually with the use of symbolic material to communicate with intention, or bodily through changes in one's behavioral state, which may serve a nonintentional communicative function, as noted with observation of Chan's behavior. The other to whom one responds would most obviously include the physical presence of a human being but not necessarily so. The other could include something in nature, a memory, or an email message. In each case, to image God is to respond to the world around us. As such, *imago Dei* is a communal concept that cannot be limited to a particular, "essential" capacity possessed by an individual.

Would any and all relationships, including abusive ones, count as instances of relationships of mutual responsiveness? Could the responsiveness I describe in this project include the abusive, violent behavior of an angry spouse or the abuse of power perpetrated by a pedophile? There is an ethical question that arises when one considers human being in terms of participation in relationships of mutual responsiveness: Is participation in abusive relationships included in those mutually responsive relationships that define our humanity? I say no; abusive relationships are not included among those mutually responsive relationships that define our humanity, and it is with the help of Buber's dialogical philosophy that I make this claim. As I have discussed, for Buber it is through participation in relationships in which I respond to the Other without the objectifying, reflective functions of the I of I-It relations that I find my humanity. Thus, when I engage the Other merely as an object of my own selfish, perspectival, objectifying functions—as in the example of an adult who views a child merely as an object for the satisfaction of his or her own needs—not only am I sacrificing my own humanity, but I am also substituting the humanity of the Other for the fulfillment of my needs. When I engage the Other without the reflective, categorizing, perspectival functions of I of I-It relations, however, I am engaging the Other as it is in itself. As a result, Buber claims, not only do I find the fullness of my own humanity, but I also acknowledge the fullness of the humanity of the Other to whom I respond.

As I indicated in Chapter 4, an individual like Chan would be more apt, not less, to engage the other in this humanizing way. As a result of his intellectual disability, the objectifying, perspectival functions of the self are not available to him, and thus responding to the other in a less objectifying way is more accessible to him and individuals like him. Granted, Chan's intellectual disability would prevent him from participation in responsive relations with great complexity. But while the intellectual capacity to employ symbolic material affords one the opportunity for relationships of such complexity, it is also accompanied by the risk of objectifying the other in destructive, abusive ways. My point here is that for individuals like Chan, the inability to employ the symbols of self and other, while limiting their capacity for certain types of complex responsive relations, also eliminates the risk of engaging in behavior that objectifies the world. They are able to participate in responsive relations through bodily changes, such as changes in their behavioral state, and yet without the objectifying functions that often result in the abuse of the other to whom one responds.

This means that the concept of the human that I am proposing, with Buber's help, is not inclusive of those relationships that are merely selfish, focusing primarily on the perspectival needs of the self. It is not inclusive of the individual whose behavior engages the Other in abusive, objectifying ways. Rather, it is inclusive of those who participate in relationships in which the Other is engaged as it is in itself, freed from our objectification of it. The important point here for the purposes of this book is that such an anthropology is broad enough to recognize the full humanity of individuals like Chan, for whom objectification of and reflection upon that which exists outside the self is not a possibility, but responsiveness to the Other without these intellectual activities is.

To conceive of the *imago Dei* in human being in similar terms—as responsiveness to the world, with or without the use of symbolic material—opens up the concept of the image of God to include not only those with the intellectual ability to communicate with the use of symbolic material but also those who respond to the world around them in nonsymbolic ways. Conversely, to limit our understanding of the *imago Dei* so as to include only those individuals with the intellectual ability to employ symbolic material, to understand and love God, or to respond obediently to God's commandments is to employ a theological concept that discriminates against those individuals with profound intellectual disabilities.

In this book, I want to avoid such discrimination and reconstruct a theological anthropology that is mindful of the full humanity of individuals with profound intellectual disabilities. I employ Kaufman's criterion of constructing theological concepts that are appropriate to a broad range of human situations, including in particular the situation of individuals with profound intellectual disabilities, and thus provide an understanding of human life that is meaningful.

There are other questions that may arise for the reader about the relevance of my theological anthropology for other groups. As I mentioned in the introduction, one may wonder about the application of my understanding of human being to individuals with limited levels of consciousness. This topic is extraordinarily complex, as there are numerous levels of consciousness identified by the medical community. Some helpful resources for understanding the variety of levels of consciousness include the Glasgow coma scale and the Rancho Los Amigos scale.[55] The Glasgow coma scale is a standardized system for measuring the level of consciousness of brain-injured individuals based on three categories: eye opening, verbal response, and motor response. The Rancho Los Amigos scale is a tool for assessing the level of an individual's brain function in the first weeks following a brain injury. It involves eight levels based on observation of the individual's response to external stimuli. Although every brain-injured person is unique, as is his or her recovery, these standardized tests are helpful resources for understanding a very complex set of neurological signs and symptoms.

I am reminded here of Terry Schiavo, who, after suffering an anoxic event in 1990, emerged from a coma into a vegetative state in which she remained until her death in 2005. Her case received widespread media attention in the United States as her family struggled through the court system with divergent positions on whether or not to continue life-supporting procedures. As I see it, the question with regard to Terry Schiavo has less to do with her level of responsiveness and more to do with what levels of responsiveness we consider to be evidence of a life worth living. Why is it that we often question the value of those who, either by birth or by accident later in life, are unable to respond with higher levels of cognitive activity? As it turns out, evaluation of Terry Schiavo's behavior indicates that she possessed the capacity to vocalize purposefully and communicate symbolically, although doubts about the accuracy of this evaluation ultimately resulted in her death.[56]

My point in this book has been that symbolic levels of responsiveness should not be the indicator of a life worth living. I hope that through the course of this work I have raised awareness of the bias in our society toward intellectual ability that, I believe, is the primary reason why we question the value of these individuals. There is much more work to be done to raise awareness of the responsiveness of individuals with varying levels of consciousness and their value in the church and society, and I hope that this book will provoke an interest in others to pursue this topic of research further.

Another area for further exploration includes the relevance of my thesis for animals. If, as I suggest, we broaden the concept human being to include nonsymbolic modes of responsiveness, could animals be included in this concept? If human being is no longer limited to those individuals with the intellectual capacity to understand God, respond obediently to God's commandments, or engage symbols of self and other as they respond to the world around them, and if the concept of the human is broadened to include nonsymbolic, more bodily ways of responding, why would animals not be included among those creatures considered human?[57] My initial response is to question the desire to distinguish humans from animals in the first place. It seems to me that this desire to define what sets humans apart from the rest of creation stems from an anthropocentrism that has fueled the denigration and destruction of nonhuman creatures for centuries. And the historical emphasis on rationality as that which separates the human from the nonhuman has led to the marginalization and dehumanization of all beings considered irrational, including not only animals and inanimate beings, but women and individuals with intellectual disabilities as well.

Thus, the theological anthropology I am proposing challenges not only the emphasis on rationality as that which defines human being, but also the traditional distinction between the human and the nonhuman. It problematizes the separating uses to which the concept "human being" has traditionally been put. It is an attempt to undo the separation and exclusivity that has resulted from reification of the concept and open it up to more continuity between realms. I am suggesting here that "human being" should be used to name not only those beings with intellectual capacities, but those without intellectual capacities as well. And because the term has historically been used to identify those beings considered worthy of care and respect, broadening the meaning of the term to include responsiveness to the world in both nonsymbolic and symbolic ways results in an ethic of care that demands respect for the dignity and value of all creatures, and not just those with intellectual capacities.

Thus, this theological anthropology could support an environmental ethic that promotes the protection of nature's resources from destruction for the purposes of human greed and financial gain. It could support an animal rights ethic that seeks to protect animals from extinction as a result of the human desire to control their habitat. It could support a feminist ethic that promotes equal rights for all people, regardless of gender, race, religious affiliation, sexual orientation, and the like. It could support a disability rights ethic that protects individuals with all types of disabilities from discrimination on the basis of their disability. And it could support a children's rights ethic that protects the rights of children of all ages to be raised in an environment that is free of abuse and neglect. This theological anthropology that I am proposing clearly complicates what it means to be made in the image of God; by broadening its meaning to include responsiveness in both nonsymbolic and symbolic modes, it greatly broadens the range of those creatures considered human. It also results in a more demanding ethic of care, whereby social policies and personal practices are required that respect the dignity of all creatures, and not just those considered rational or intellectually gifted. It puts much heavier demands on us to act in ways that are mindful of the value of all creation and of the Christian claim that, because God created all things, all created things image God. It is my hope that by complicating the meaning of "human being," this theological anthropology will further the growing interest in acknowledging the value of individuals with profound intellectual disabilities around us, including the value of all of God's creation.

NOTES

INTRODUCTION

1. Fred Pelka, *The ABC-CLIO Companion to the Disability Rights Movement* (Santa Barbara, Calif.: ABC-CLIO, 1997), 190–191, 215–217, 236–237.

2. Diane Driedger, *The Last Civil Rights Movement: Disabled Peoples' International* (New York: St. Martin's, 1989), 4.

3. Robert Funk, "Disability Rights: From Caste to Class in the Context of Civil Rights," in *Images of the Disabled, Disabling Images*, ed. Alan Gartner and Tom Joe (New York: Praeger, 1987), 7–8.

4. Pelka, *ABC-CLIO Companion*, 18–22, 262–264.

5. Nancy L. Eiesland, *The Disabled God: Toward a Liberatory Theology of Disability* (Nashville, Tenn.: Abingdon Press, 1994).

6. Ibid., 27.

7. Thomas E. Reynolds, *Vulnerable Communion: A Theology of Disability and Hospitality* (Grand Rapids, Mich.: Brazos Press, 2008), 12, 27.

8. Ibid., 14.

9. Ibid., 103.

10. Ibid.,

11. Ibid., 107.

12. Ibid., 120–123.

13. Ibid., 182.

14. Ibid., 183.

15. Ibid., 124–127.

16. Amos Yong, *Theology and Down Syndrome: Reimagining Disability in Late Modernity* (Waco, Tex.: Baylor University Press, 2007), 11–12.

17. Ibid., 11–13.

18. Ibid., 184–185.

19. Ibid., 188.

20. Ibid., 187–188.

21. Ibid., 187.

22. Hans S. Reinders, *Receiving the Gift of Friendship: Profound Disability, Theological Anthropology and Ethics* (Grand Rapids, Mich.: Eerdmans, 2008).

23. Ibid., 244.

24. Ibid., 44.

25. Ibid., 244.

26. Ibid.

27. Reynolds, *Vulnerable Communion*, 123–129.

28. Yong, *Theology and Down Syndrome*, 187–188.

29. Ibid.

30. Ibid., 271.

31. Ibid., 244.

32. Ibid., 270–271.

33. Ibid., 313.

34. Ibid., 244.

35. Ibid., 228.

36. Ibid., 244.

37. Gordon Kaufman, *God the Problem* (Cambridge, Mass.: Harvard University Press, 1972), xii.

38. Paul Arthur Schilpp and Maurice Friedman, eds., *The Philosophy of Martin Buber* (LaSalle, Ill.: Open Court, 1967), 103.

39. Eiesland, *The Disabled God*, 52.

40. Ibid.

41. Ibid., 52–53.

42. Ibid., 66.

43. Deborah Creamer, *Disability and Christian Theology: Embodied Limits and Constructive Possibilities* (New York: Oxford University Press, 2009), 32.

44. Ibid., 31.

45. Ibid., 32.

46. Ellin Siegel and Amy Wetherby, "Nonsymbolic Communication," in *Instruction of Students with Severe Disability*, ed. Martha E. Snell and Fredda Brown (Upper Saddle River, N.J.: Prentice-Hall, 2000). The theory of nonsymbolic communication Siegel and Wetherby employ has been helpful in my conception of individuals with profound intellectual disabilities as participators in relationship, as communicators and responders in a nonsymbolic way.

47. Martin Buber, *I and Thou*, trans. Ronald Gregor Smith (Edinburgh: T&T Clark, 1958), 89.

48. Elizabeth A. Johnson, *She Who Is: The Mystery of God in Feminist Theological Discourse* (New York: Crossroad, 1992).

49. Eiesland, *The Disabled God*, 86–87.

1. GORDON KAUFMAN: HUMAN BEING AS INTENTIONAL AGENT

1. Gordon Kaufman, *An Essay on Theological Method*, 3rd ed. (Atlanta, Ga.: Scholars Press, 1995), 36.

2. Ibid., 35.

3. Ibid., xx.

4. Ibid., 40.

5. Ibid.

6. Ibid.

7. Gordon Kaufman, *In Face of Mystery* (Cambridge, Mass.: Harvard University Press, 1993), 103.

8. Ibid., 105.

9. Ibid., 108.

10. Ibid., 103.

11. Serene Jones, *Feminist Theory and Christian Theology: Cartographies of Grace* (Minneapolis: Augsburg Fortress, 2000), 25.

12. Ibid., 29.

13. The concept of strategic essentialism, or "the risk of essence," was first associated with the feminist critic Gayatri Chakravorty Spivak. See Gayatri Chakravorty Spivak, *In Other Worlds: Essays in Cultural Politics* (New York: Methuen, 1987), 204–205.

14. Jones, *Feminist Theory and Christian Theology*, 43–48.

15. Gordon Kaufman, *Systematic Theology: A Historicist Perspective* (New York: Charles Scribner's Sons, 1968), 33.

16. Ibid.

17. Ibid., 34.

18. Ibid.

19. Ibid., 39.

20. Ibid.

21. Ibid., 40.

22. Though the requirement of symbolization for defining human being remains implicit in Kaufman's *Systematic Theology*, as will soon be discussed, it appears explicitly and fully developed in *In Face of Mystery*.

23. There is often a circular pattern to the relationship between Kaufman's anthropology and his doctrine of God. In his *Systematic Theology*, Kaufman employs the finite model of the human as an agent for imaging God. This is an acceptable theological move. As noted at the beginning of this chapter, Kaufman himself admits that the theologian does not have direct access to God in God's transcendence. It is acceptable to employ finite models (emphasis on the plural) in an effort to express what cannot be expressed another way. This model then reappears here as Kaufman employs it to define what is essential to human being, through the doctrine of the *imago Dei*. This second move is a problematic one commonly made in theological anthropology—locating what is essential to human being based on an understanding of God that is imagined by appeal to a limited model of the human being.

24. Kaufman, *Systematic Theology*, 329.

25. Ibid., 332.

26. Ibid., 334–335.

27. Ibid., 344.

28. Ibid.

29. Kaufman, *In Face of Mystery*, 103.

30. Ibid., 101.

31. Ibid., 102.

32. Ibid., 103. As noted previously, Kaufman's claim that human beings are fundamentally historical beings is important for my critique of his anthropology. It is not the case that human beings are one historical being among other historical beings. Rather, according to Kaufman, this capacity for self-creation is what defines human being; it is what distinguishes human being from other living beings. Ibid., 105.

33. Ibid., 104.

34. Ibid., 103.

35. Ibid., 106.

36. Ibid., 109.

37. Ibid.

38. Ibid., 143.

39. Ibid., 144–145, 148–149. The premise, Kaufman claims, of all liberation theologies that seek to protect the oppressed from social structures that prevent them from exercising their capacity for agency is "that our agency, as I have been arguing here, is a central feature of our humanity."

40. Ibid., 150.

41. Ibid., 152.

42. Ibid., 152–153.

43. Ibid., 153.

44. Ibid., 150.

45. Ibid., 146.

46. Ibid., 157.

47. Ibid., 160.

48. Ibid., 159.

49. Ibid., 160–161.

50. Ibid., 161.

51. Kaufman's claim that language and the structure of society are required in the development of the self as agent is not being contested here. I agree with Kaufman that as languages and societies grow in complexity, so do opportunities for the exercise of agency, as a greater variety of choices become available. What I am contesting, however, is this claim, alongside Kaufman's earlier claim that human being is defined by one's capacity for agency. This leads one to conclude that individuals without language ability, and thus without agency, are deficiently human.

52. Kaufman, *Systematic Theology*, 344.

53. Kaufman, *In Face of Mystery*, 146.

54. Ibid., 161. See also 105, 109.

55. Kaufman, *An Essay on Theological Method*, 42.

56. Kaufman, *Systematic Theology*, 344.

57. Kaufman, *An Essay on Theological Method*, 40.

58. Paul Arthur Schilpp and Maurice Friedman, eds., *The Philosophy of Martin Buber* (LaSalle, Ill.: Open Court, 1967), 103.

59. Ibid., 71; see also 97–99.

60. Ibid., 78.

61. Ibid., 105–157.

2. GEORGE LINDBECK: HUMAN BEING AS
LANGUAGE USER

1. George A. Lindbeck, *The Nature of Doctrine: Religion and Theology in a Postliberal Age* (Philadelphia: Westminster Press, 1984), 8–9.

2. Ibid., 8, 18.

3. Ibid., 16.

4. Ibid., 16, 17.

5. Ibid., 19–25.

6. Clifford Geertz, *The Interpretation of Cultures* (New York: Basic Books, 1973), 44.

7. Lindbeck, *The Nature of Doctrine*, 33.

8. Ibid., 18.

9. Ibid., 25.

10. Ibid., 30.

11. Bernard Lonergan, *Method in Theology* (New York: Herder and Herder, 1972), 101–124.

12. Ibid., 105, 120.

13. Lindbeck, *The Nature of Doctrine*, 31.

14. Ibid., 31–32.

15. Ibid.

16. Ibid., 31–33.

17. Ibid., 33, 34.

18. Ibid., 34.

19. Ibid., 36, 37.

20. I use "symbolic material" in the way that Lindbeck uses "signs and symbols" and Geertz uses "significant symbols": as a reference to those public gestures, words, actions, and so forth that are used with the intent to give meaning to experience. Ibid., 38; Geertz, *Interpretation of Cultures*, 45.

21. Lindbeck, *The Nature of Doctrine*, 38.

22. Ludwig Wittgenstein, *Zettel*, ed. G. E. M. Anscombe and G. H. von Wright (Berkeley: University of California Press, 1967), #529, 95e.

23. Ludwig Wittgenstein, *Philosophical Investigations*, 3rd ed. (Oxford: Blackwell, 2001), #293, 100e.

24. Ibid., 373, 116e.

25. Ibid., 293, 100e.

26. My reading of Wittgenstein accords with that of John W. Cook, "Human Being," in *Studies in the Philosophy of Wittgenstein*, ed. Peter Winch, 144–149 (New York: Humanities Press, 1969).

27. Wittgenstein, *Philosophical Investigations*, #304, 102e.

28. Cook, "Human Being," 145.

29. Ibid.

30. Lindbeck, *The Nature of Doctrine*, 37–38.

31. Ibid., 37.

32. Cook, "Human Being," 145.

33. Ibid., 142.

34. Wittgenstein, *Zettel*, #529, 95; #540, 95e.

35. Ibid., 545, 96e; #541, 95e.

36. Wittgenstein, *Philosophical Investigations*, #244, 89e.

37. Lindbeck, *The Nature of Doctrine*, 33–34, 40–42.

38. Ibid., 33–34.

39. Cook, "Human Being," 147.

40. Stanley Hauerwas, "The Gesture of a Truthful Story," in *Critical Reflections on Stanley Hauerwas' Theology of Disability: Disabling Society, Enabling Theology*, ed. John Swinton (Birmingham, N.Y.: Haworth Pastoral Press, 2004), 72.

41. Ibid.

42. Ibid., 72–73.

43. Ibid.

44. Ibid., 73.

45. Ibid., 79.

46. Ibid., 77.

47. Hauerwas may answer this question with the claim that the gestures *are* the story: "to be Christian is to kneel," and so on. This response would be fitting for individuals with abled bodies, for whom kneeling poses no difficulty. However, most individuals with profound intellectual disabilities present with severe physical disabilities as well. The discrimination here would be doubled. Not only would they be excluded from learning the story based on their intellectual disability, but these individuals would also be excluded based on their physical disabilities.

48. See Sheila Greeve Davaney, *Pragmatic Historicism: A Theology for the Twenty-First Century* (Albany: State University of New York Press, 2000), 23.

49. Ibid., 29–47.

50. Ibid., 38.

3. HUMAN BEING IN RELATIONAL TERMS:
A PHENOMENOLOGY

1. "Intellectual disability" is a newly emerging term that seems to be preferred by people who have traditionally been referred to as "mentally retarded." I use the term

to refer to people with mental retardation, particularly profound mental retardation. I use "intellectual disability" as distinct from "cognitive disability," which includes learning disabilities, Alzheimer's disease, and the like. I also avoid the term "mental disability," for it is unclear whether it refers to intellectual disabilities, cognitive disabilities, or what some call psychiatric or mental health disabilities. This information is based on email correspondence with H. Stephen Kaye, Research Director, Disability Statistics Center at the Institute for Health and Aging at the University of California, San Francisco.

2. George Lindbeck, *The Nature of Doctrine: Religion and Theology in a Postliberal Age* (Philadelphia: Westminster Press, 1984), 38.

3. Robert E. Wood, ed., *Martin Buber's Ontology: An Analysis of I and Thou* (Evanston, Ill.: Northwestern University Press, 1969), 52–61. I am aware that Levinasians will worry about the term "totalization." For Levinas, "totality" denotes comprehensive knowledge of the Other and the reduction of the Other to the same. Thus, it is important to note that the sense in which Wood speaks of the "totalization" characteristic of the I-Thou relation is very different from Levinas's use of the term. For Wood, the totalization of Buber's I-Thou relation involves not comprehensive knowledge of the Other but the encounter of the Other as a whole, without reflective attention to its particular aspects. Buber does speak of what we experience in I-Thou encounter as "Just everything. For we know nothing isolated about it any more." However, we must understand this as a rhetorical flourish, given his consistent expression of the I-Thou encounter as involving meeting the Other as it is in itself, freed from the subjective, perspectival functions of the I. Martin Buber, *I and Thou*, trans. Ronald Gregor Smith (Edinburgh: T&T Clark, 1958), 11.

4. Martin Buber, *Das Problem des Menschen* (Heidelberg: Lambert Schneider, 1954), 169.

5. Ellen Siegel and Amy Wetherby, "Nonsymbolic Communication," in *Instruction of Students with Severe Disability* (Upper Saddle River, N.J.: Prentice-Hall, 2000), 413–414. They employ this model as developed by E. Bates and associates in *The Emergence of Symbols: Cognition and Communication in Infancy* (New York: Academic Press, 1979).

6. Siegel and Wetherby, "Nonsymbolic Communication," 441.

7. Ibid., 413–414.

8. Ibid., 414.

9. Ibid., 427. Siegel and Wetherby define intentionality as "the deliberate pursuit of a goal. Behavior is intentional if an individual has an awareness or mental representation of the desired goal as well as the means to obtain the goal." Ibid., 415.

10. Ibid., 413–415.

11. Gordon Kaufman, *In Face of Mystery* (Cambridge, Mass.: Harvard University Press, 1993), 157.

12. Michael B. First, ed., "Disorders Usually First Diagnosed in Infancy, Childhood, or Adolescence," *Diagnostic and Statistical Manual—Text Revision* (DSM-IV-TR, 2000), http://online.statref.com/document.aspx?fxid=37&docid=13.

13. Adaptive behavior refers to "how effectively individuals cope with common life demands and how well they meet the standards of personal independence expected of someone in their particular group, sociocultural background, and community setting." Ibid.

14. A behavioral state and changes in behavioral state are not learned responses. A behavioral state is a manifestation of the physiological condition of an individual that can be facilitated through changes in external variables, such as social contact, body position, type of activity and the activity level of the immediate environment. Siegel and Wetherby, "Nonsymbolic Communication," 433.

15. A "mat" refers to a padded table common to a physical therapy gym on which an average-sized adult can sit with his or her feet flat on the floor.

16. Siegel and Wetherby, "Nonsymbolic Communication," 414–415.

4. MARTIN BUBER'S ANTHROPOLOGY

1. Ludwig Feuerbach, *Grundsätze der Philosophie der Zukunft* (Leipzig, 1847).

2. Robert E. Wood, *Martin Buber's Ontology: An Analysis of I and Thou* (Evanston, Ill.: Northwestern University Press, 1969), 5.

3. Michael Theunissen, *The Other: Studies in the Social Ontology of Husserl, Heidegger, Sartre, and Buber*, trans. Christopher Macann (Cambridge, Mass.: MIT Press, 1984), 266.

4. Paul Arthur Schilpp and Maurice Friedman, eds., *The Philosophy of Martin Buber* (Lasalle, Ill.: Open Court Press, 1967), 115.

5. Ibid., 693.

6. Martin Buber, *Between Man and Man* (New York: Macmillan, 1965), 124.

7. Ibid., 22–23; Wood, *Martin Buber's Ontology*, 37.

8. Martin Buber, *I and Thou*, trans. Ronald Gregor Smith (Edinburgh: T&T Clark, 1958), 16; Wood, *Martin Buber's Ontology*, 39.

9. Wood, *Martin Buber's Ontology*, 39.

10. Theunissen, *The Other*, 273.

11. Wood, *Martin Buber's Ontology*, 39.

12. Buber, *I and Thou*, 31.

13. Ibid., 17–18; Wood, *Martin Buber's Ontology*, 41.

14. There is a special sense in which I-Thou names a relation that is non-objectifying and relational in the true and genuine sense. The I-It can also be called "relation," but it is obviously a deficient or instrumental mode of relation; it does not rise to what Buber means by relational in its fullest sense. When I use the term relation or relationality, I am referring specifically to the I-Thou relation.

15. Ibid., 25. Theunissen clarifies that the "means" to which Buber refers is used not only in the sense of "means to an end," to indicate that the Thou is not a means to be used for the ends of the I. "Means" is also used here to indicate a medium, in the sense of a concept that "fixes beings with a determinate sense

and orders them into the system of unified signs." Buber rejects any "means" in this sense as an obstruction of the immediate I-Thou relation. Theunissen, *The Other*, 275.

16. Wood, *Martin Buber's Ontology*, 54–55.

17. Buber, *I and Thou*, 40–44. Buber considers the prenatal and early postnatal child as examples of individuals who participate in these relations of unmediated presence. See also Buber, *Between Man and Man*, 98.

18. Ibid., 44–50.

19. Alfred Schutz and Thomas Luckmann, *The Structures of the Life-World*, trans. Richard M. Zaner and H. Tristram Engelhardt Jr. (Evanston, Ill.: Northwestern University Press, 1973), 64.

20. Ibid., 62.

21. Ibid., 64.

22. Richard M. Zaner, *The Context of Self: A Phenomenological Inquiry Using Medicine as a Clue* (Athens: Ohio University Press, 1981), 227.

23. Schutz and Luckman, *The Structures of the Life-World*, 64.

24. Ibid.

25. Wood, *Martin Buber's Ontology*, 52.

26. Buber, *I and Thou*, 32–37; Wood, *Martin Buber's Ontology*, 53.

27. Buber, *I and Thou*, 24.

28. Ibid.

29. Theunissen, *The Other*, 280.

30. Buber, *I and Thou*, 20; Wood, *Martin Buber's Ontology*, 53.

31. Martin Buber, *Die Schriften über Das Dialogische Prinzip* (Heidelberg: Verlag Lambert Schneider, 1954), 15; Theunissen, *The Other*, 280.

32. Theunissen, *The Other*, 280.

33. Buber, *I and Thou*, 30.

34. Ibid., 28–29.

35. Wood, *Martin Buber's Ontology*, 60.

36. Buber, *I and Thou*, 29.

37. Wood, *Martin Buber's Ontology*, 61.

38. Buber, *Hasidism and Modern Man*, 33.

39. Buber, *I and Thou*, 30.

40. Ibid.

41. Buber uses "dialogue" metaphorically to refer to the I-Thou relation as that which rises above the plane of linguistic expressions. Of course, to speak of metaphor here may be misleading. For Buber, dialogue is much more than merely metaphor. It is a way of speaking of a living relation that takes place in the encounter between I and Thou.

42. Buber, *Between Man and Man*, 10.

43. Schilpp and Friedman, *The Philosophy of Martin Buber*, 99.

44. Buber, *Between Man and Man*, 16.

45. Schilpp and Friedman, *The Philosophy of Martin Buber*, 100.

46. Buber, *Between Man and Man*, 45.

47. Schilpp and Friedman, *The Philosophy of Martin Buber*, 100.

48. Theunissen, *The Other*, 286.

49. Buber, *Die Schriften*, 32.

50. Theunissen, *The Other*, 286.

51. Buber, *I and Thou*, 15.

52. Ibid., 85–88.

53. Wood, *Martin Buber's Ontology*, 81.

54. Buber, *I and Thou*, 85–88.

55. Buber, *Die Schriften*, 32.

56. Wood, *Martin Buber's Ontology*, 82.

57. Buber, *Die Schriften*, 32.

58. Theunissen, *The Other*, 286–287.

59. Sydney and Beatrice Rome, eds., *Philosophical Interrogations* (New York: Harper & Row, 1964), 36.

60. Ibid. See also Buber, *I and Thou*, 40–44; *Between Man and Man*, 98.

61. Ibid., 25–26.

62. Ibid., 44–50.

63. Wood, *Martin Buber's Ontology*, 52.

64. Buber, *I and Thou*, 24, 30.

65. Wood, *Martin Buber's Ontology*, 52.

66. Buber, *I and Thou*, 31.

67. Wood, *Martin Buber's Ontology*, 52.

68. Buber, *Between Man and Man*, 96–101.

69. Ibid., 96–97, 100–101.

70. Theunissen, *The Other*, 280.

71. Buber, *I and Thou*, 24.

72. Ibid., 24.

73. Wood, *Martin Buber's Ontology*, 53.

74. Buber, *I and Thou*, 20.

75. Ibid., 30.

76. Ibid. See also *Between Man and Man*, "Education," 83–103, and "The Education of Character," 104–117.

77. Ibid., 29.

78. Ibid.

79. L'Arche communities bring together people, some with developmental disabilities and some without, who choose to share their lives by living together in ecumenical, faith-based communities. From the original community, founded by Jean Vanier in France in 1964, 120 other communities have been founded throughout the world in Europe, Africa, Asia, and the Americas.

80. Jean Vanier, *The Heart of L'Arche* (Toronto: Novalis, 1995), 32–33.

81. Ibid., 32.

82. Ibid., 34–35.

83. Ibid., 35–36.

84. Ibid., 23–51.

85. Buber, *Between Man and Man*, 106.

86. Ibid., 105.

87. Vanier, *The Heart of L'Arche*, 39–40.

88. Buber, *Die Schriften*, 32.

89. Schilpp and Friedman, *The Philosophy of Martin Buber*, 99.

90. Buber, *I and Thou*, 18–20, 24.

91. Theunissen, *The Other*, 286–287.

92. Buber, *I and Thou*, 31.

93. Ibid., 85–88.

5. *IMAGO DEI* AS RATIONALITY OR RELATIONALITY: HISTORY AND CONSTRUCTION

1. Douglas John Hall, *Imaging God: Dominion as Stewardship* (Grand Rapids, Mich.: Eerdmans, 1986), 61.

2. Cuthbert A. Simpson, *The Interpreter's Bible* (New York: Abingdon Press, 1952), 1:484. See also Tikvah Frymer-Kensky's interpretation of the image of God in terms of physical resemblance: Tikva Frymer-Kensky, Peter Ochs, David Novak, Michael Singer, and David Fox Sandmel, *Christianity in Jewish Terms (Radical Traditions)* (Boulder: Westview Press, 2000), 321.

3. G. C. Berkouwer, *Man: The Image of God*, trans. Dirk W. Jellema (Grand Rapids, Mich.: Eerdmans, 1962), 70ff.

4. Hall, *Imaging God*, 71–72.

5. Paul Ramsey, *Basic Christian Ethics* (New York: Charles Scribner's Sons, 1950).

6. Hall, *Imaging God*, 89.

7. Ramsey, *Basic Christian Ethics*, 250.

8. Hall, *Imaging God*, 90.

9. Hendrikus Berkhof, *Christian Faith: An Introduction to the Study of the Faith*, trans. Sierd Woudstra (Grand Rapids, Mich.: Eerdmans, 1979), 179.

10. Hall, *Imaging God*, 91–92.

11. Ramsey, *Basic Christian Ethics*, 250–264.

12. David Cairns, *The Image of God in Man* (London: SCM Press, 1973), 125.

13. Hall, *Imaging God*, 100.

14. Ibid., 493.

15. Ibid., 492–493.

16. Ibid.

17. Ibid., 494.

18. Ibid., 495.

19. Anthony A. Hoekema, *Created in God's Image* (Grand Rapids, Mich.: Eerdmans, 1986), 37.

20. Aquinas clarifies what he means by "mind" when he speaks of "the acts of the mind" as thinking that forms an internal word from the knowledge we possess. Thomas Aquinas, *The Summa Theologica*, ed. Clifton Fadiman and Philip W. Goetz, trans. Father Laurence Shapcote (Chicago: Encyclopaedia Britannica, 1990), 1:498.

21. Ibid., 494.

22. Ibid.

23. John Calvin, *Institutes of the Christian Religion*, vol. 1, ed. John T. McNeill, trans. Ford Lewis Battles (Philadelphia: Westminster Press, 1960), 184–186.

24. Ibid., 185.

25. Cairns, *The Image of God in Man*, 135.

26. John Calvin, *Commentary on the Book of Psalms*, trans. James Anderson (Grand Rapids, Mich.: Eerdmans, 1949), 1:308–333.

27. Ibid.

28. Hall, *Imaging God*, 102.

29. John Calvin, *Commentary on the First Book of Moses Called Genesis*, vol. 1 (Edinburgh: Calvin Translation Society, 1847), 93.

30. Ibid., 94.

31. John Calvin, *Institutes of the Christian Religion*, vol. 1, trans. John Allen (Philadelphia: Presbyterian Board of Christian Education, n.d.), 210.

32. John Calvin, *Commentaries on the Four Last Books of Moses*, vol. 1, trans. Charles William Bingham (Grand Rapids, Mich.: Eerdmans, 1950), 349.

33. Calvin, *Commentary on the Book of Psalms*, 308–309.

34. Cairns, *The Image of God in Man*, 137.

35. Hall, *Imaging God*, 104.

36. Calvin, *Institutes*, 208.

37. Hall, *Imaging God*, 104.

38. Ibid.

39. Ibid., 208.

40. Hall, *Imaging God*, 104.

41. Ibid.

42. T. F. Torrance, *Calvin's Doctrine of Man* (Grand Rapids, Mich.: Eerdmans, 1957), 91.

43. Ramsey, *Basic Christian Ethics*, 255.

44. Hall, *Imaging God*, 106.

45. Cairns, *The Image of God in Man*, 137.

46. Exodus 17:1–7.

47. Gordon Kaufman, *In Face of Mystery* (Cambridge, Mass.: Harvard University Press, 1993), 271.

48. Ibid.

49. Ibid., 270.

50. Ibid., 272.

51. Ibid., 270.

52. Pseudo-Dionysius, "The Divine Names," in *Pseudo-Dionysius: The Complete Works*, trans. Colm Luibheid (New York: Paulist Press, 1987), 82.

53. Ibid.

54. Ibid., 82–83.

55. For a description of both scales, see Darcy Ann Umphred, *Neurological Rehabilitation* (St. Louis: Mosby, 1995), 421, 427.

56. For details of this evaluation, see the affidavit of Terry Schiavo's speech-language pathologist before the Sixth Judicial Circuit Court for Pinellas County, Florida, Probate Division, File No. 90-2908GD-003, on September 17, 2003, or see http://abstractappeal.com/schiavo/trialctorder0903.pdf.

57. On the relationality of animals, see works by the Dutch primatologist and ethologist Frans B. M. de Waal, especially *The Age of Empathy: Nature's Lessons for a Kinder Society* (New York: Harmony Books, 2009) and *Chimpanzee Politics: Power and Sex Among Apes* (Baltimore: Johns Hopkins University Press, 1998). See also Temple Grandin, *Animals in Translation: Using the Mysteries of Autism to Decode Animal Behavior* (New York: Scribner, 2005), and, with Catherine Johnson, *Animals Make Us Human: Creating the Best Life for Animals* (Orlando, Fla.: Houghton Mifflin Harcourt, 2009).

BIBLIOGRAPHY

Albrecht, Gary L., ed. *The Sociology of Physical Disability and Rehabilitation*. Pittsburgh: University of Pittsburgh Press, 1976.

Aquinas, St. Thomas. *The Summa Theologica. Volume I*. Edited by Clifton Fadiman and Philip W. Goetz. Translated by Father Laurence Shapcote. Chicago: Encyclopaedia Britannica, 1990.

Bates, E. *The Emergence of Symbols: Cognition and Communication in Infancy*. New York: Academic Press, 1979.

Berkhof, Hendrikus. *Christian Faith: An Introduction to the Study of the Faith*. Translated by Sierd Woudstra. Grand Rapids, Mich.: Eerdmans, 1979.

Berkouwer, G. C. *Man: The Image of God*. Translated by Dirk W. Jellema. Grand Rapids, Mich.: Eerdmans, 1962.

Buber, Martin. *Between Man and Man*. Translated by Ronald Gregor Smith. Boston: Beacon Press, 1955.

———. *Das Problem des Menschen*. Heidelberg: Lambert Schneider, 1954.

———. *Die Schriften über das Dialogische Prinzip*. Heidelberg: Verlag Lambert Schneider, 1954.

———. *Hasidism and Modern Man*. Atlantic Highlands, N.J.: Humanities Press, 1980.

———. *I and Thou*. Translated by Ronald Gregor Smith. Edinburgh: T&T Clark, 1958.

Cairns, David. *The Image of God in Man*. London: Collins Clear-Type Press, 1973.

Calvin, John. *Commentary on the Book of Psalms*. Translated by James Anderson. Grand Rapids, Mich.: Eerdmans, 1949.

———. *Commentary on the First Book of Moses Called Genesis. Volume I*. Edinburgh: Calvin Translation Society, 1847.

———. *Commentary on the Four Last Books of Moses. Volume I*. Translated by Charles William Bingham. Grand Rapids, Mich.: William B. Eerdmans, 1950.

———. *Institutes of the Christian Religion. Volume I*. Edited by John T. McNeil. Translated by Ford Lewis Battles. Philadelphia: Westminster Press, 1960.

———. *Institutes of the Christian Religion. Volume I.* Translated by John Allen. Philadelphia: Presbyterian Board of Christian Education, n.d.

Creamer, Deborah. *Disability and Christian Theology: Embodied Limits and Constructive Possibilities.* New York: Oxford University Press, 2009.

Davaney, Sheila Greeve. *Pragmatic Historicism: A Theology for the Twenty-first Century.* Albany: State University of New York Press, 2000.

DeWaal, Frans. *The Age of Empathy: Nature's Lessons for a Kinder Society.* New York: Harmony Books, 2009.

———. *Chimpanzee Politics: Power and Sex Among Apes.* Baltimore: Johns Hopkins University Press, 1998.

Driedger, Diane. *The Last Civil Rights Movement: Disabled Peoples' International.* New York: St. Martin's Press, 1989.

Eiesland, Nancy L. *The Disabled God: Toward a Liberatory Theology of Disability.* Nashville: Abingdon Press, 1994.

Feuerbach, Ludwig. *Grundsätze der Philosophie der Zukunft.* Leipzig, 1847.

First, Michael B., Allen Frances, and Harold Alan Pincus, eds. *DSM-IV-TR Handbook of Differential Diagnosis.* Washington, D.C.: American Psychiatric Press, 2002.

Frymer-Kensky, Tikva, Peter Ochs, David Novak, Michael Singer, and David Fox Sandmel, eds. *Christianity in Jewish Terms.* Boulder: Westview Press, 2000.

Gartner, Alan, Tom Joe, eds. *Images of the Disabled, Disabling Images.* New York: Praeger, 1987.

Geertz, Clifford. *The Interpretation of Cultures.* New York: Basic Books, 1973.

Grandin, Temple. *Animals in Translation: Using the Mysteries of Autism to Decode Animal Behavior.* New York: Scribner, 2005.

Grandin, Temple, and Catherine Johnson. *Animals Make Us Human: Creating the Best Life for Animals.* Orlando, Fla.: Houghton Mifflin Harcourt, 2009.

Hall, Douglas John. *Imaging God: Dominion as Stewardship.* Grand Rapids, Mich.: Eerdmans, 1986.

Hoekema, Anthony A. *Created in God's Image.* Grand Rapids, Mich.: Eerdmans, 1986.

Jennett, Brian, and Graham Teasdale. *Management of Head Injuries.* Philadelphia: F. A. Davis, 1981.

Johnson, Elizabeth A. *She Who Is: The Mystery of God in Feminist Theological Discourse.* New York: Crossroad, 1992.

Jones, Serene. *Feminist Theory and Christian Theology: Cartographies of Grace.* Minneapolis: Augsburg Fortress, 2000.

Kaufman, Gordon D. *An Essay on Theological Method.* 3rd ed. Atlanta, Ga.: Scholars Press, 1995.

———. *God the Problem.* Cambridge, Mass.: Harvard University Press, 1972.

———. *In Face of Mystery.* Cambridge, Mass.: Harvard University Press, 1993.

———. *Systematic Theology: A Historicist Perspective.* New York: Scribner, 1968.

Lindbeck, George A. *The Nature of Doctrine: Religion and Theology in a Postliberal Age*. Philadelphia: Westminster Press, 1984.

Lonergan, Bernard. *Method in Theology*. New York: Herder and Herder, 1972.

Pelka, Fred. *The ABC-CLIO Companion to the Disability Rights Movement*. Santa Barbara, Calif.: ABC-CLIO, 1987.

Pseudo-Dionysius. "The Divine Names." In *Pseudo-Dionysius: The Complete Works*. Translated by Colm Luibheid. New York: Paulist Press, 1987.

Ramsey, Paul. *Basic Christian Ethics*. New York: Scribner, 1950.

Reinders, Hans. *Receiving the Gift of Friendship: Profound Disability, Theological Anthropology, and Ethics*. Grand Rapids, Mich.: Eerdmans, 2008.

Reynolds, Thomas E. *Vulnerable Communion: A Theology of Disability and Hospitality*. Grand Rapids, Mich.: Brazos Press, 2008.

Rome, Sydney, and Beatrice Rome, eds. *Philosophical Interrogations*. New York: Harper & Row, 1964.

Schilpp, Paul Arthur, and Maurice Friedman, eds. *The Philosophy of Martin Buber*. LaSalle, Ill.: Open Court, 1967.

Schutz, Alfred. *On Phenomenology and Social Relations*. Translated by Helmut R. Wagner. Chicago: University of Chicago Press, 1970.

Schutz, Alfred, and Thomas Luckman, eds. *The Structures of the Life-World. Volume 1*. Translated by Richard M. Zaner and H. Tristram Engelhardt Jr. Evanston, Ill.: Northwestern University Press, 1973.

Simpson, Cuthbert A. *The Interpreter's Bible. Volume 1*. New York: Abingdon Press, 1952.

Snell, Martha E., and Fredda Brown, eds. *Instruction of Students with Severe Disability*. Upper Saddle River, N.J.: Prentice-Hall, 2000.

Spivak, Gayatri Chakravorty. *In Other Worlds: Essays in Cultural Politics*. New York: Methuen, 1987.

Swinton, John. *Critical Reflections on Stanley Hauerwas' Theology of Disability: Disabling Society, Enabling Theology*. Binghamton, N.Y.: Haworth Pastoral Press, 2004.

Theunissen, Michael. *The Other: Studies in the Social Ontology of Husserl, Heidegger, Sartre, and Buber*. Cambridge, Mass.: MIT Press, 1984.

Torrance, T. F. *Calvin's Doctrine of Man*. Grand Rapids, Mich.: Eerdmans Press, 1957.

Umphred, Darcy Ann. *Neurological Rehabilitation*. St. Louis: Mosby, 1995.

Vanier, Jean. *The Heart of L'Arche*. Toronto: Novalis, 1995.

Winch, Peter, ed. *Studies in the Philosophy of Wittgenstein*. New York: Humanities Press, 1969.

Wittgenstein, Ludwig. *Philosophical Investigations*. 3rd ed. Translated by G. E. M. Anscombe. Oxford: Blackwell, 2001.

———. *Zettel*. Edited by G. E. M. Anscombe and G. H. von Wright. Translated by G. E. M. Anscombe. Berkeley: University of California Press, 1967.

Wood, Robert E., ed. *Martin Buber's Ontology: An Analysis of I and Thou*. Evanston, Ill.: Northwestern University Press, 1969.

Yong, Amos. *Theology and Down Syndrome: Reimagining Disability in Late Modernity*. Waco, Tex.: Baylor University Press, 2007.

Zaner, Richard M. *The Context of the Self: A Phenomenological Inquiry Using Medicine as a Clue*. Athens: Ohio University Press, 1981.